Euripides: *Iphigenia among the Taurians*

COMPANIONS TO GREEK AND ROMAN TRAGEDY

Series Editor: Thomas Harrison

Aeschylus: Agamemnon, Barbara Goward
Aeschylus: Eumenides, Robin Mitchell-Boyask
Aeschylus: Libation Bearers, C. W. Marshall
Aeschylus: Persians, David Rosenbloom
Aeschylus: Prometheus Bound, I. A. Ruffell
Aeschylus: Seven Against Thebes, Isabelle Torrance
Aeschylus: Suppliants, Thalia Papadopoulou
Euripides: Alcestis, Niall W. Slater
Euripides: Bacchae, Sophie Mills
Euripides: Cyclops, Carl A. Shaw
Euripides: Hecuba, Helene P. Foley
Euripides: Heracles, Emma Griffiths
Euripides: Hippolytus, Sophie Mills
Euripides: Ion, Laura Swift
Euripides: Iphigenia at Aulis, Pantelis Michelakis
Euripides: Medea, William Allan
Euripides: Orestes, Matthew Wright
Euripides: Phoenician Women, Thalia Papadopoulou
Euripides: Suppliant Women, Ian Storey
Euripides: Trojan Women, Barbara Goff
Seneca: Hercules Furens, Neil W. Bernstein
Seneca: Phaedra, Roland Mayer
Seneca Oedipus, Susanna Braund
Seneca: Thyestes, Peter Davis
Sophocles: Antigone, Douglas Cairns
Sophocles: Ajax, Jon Hesk
Sophocles: Electra, Michael Lloyd
Sophocles: Oedipus at Colonus, Adrian Kelly
Sophocles: Philoctetes, Hanna Roisman
Sophocles: Women of Trachis, Brad Levett

Euripides: *Iphigenia among the Taurians*

Isabelle Torrance

BLOOMSBURY ACADEMIC
LONDON • NEW YORK • OXFORD • NEW DELHI • SYDNEY

BLOOMSBURY ACADEMIC
Bloomsbury Publishing Plc
50 Bedford Square, London, WC1B 3DP, UK
1385 Broadway, New York, NY 10018, USA

BLOOMSBURY, BLOOMSBURY ACADEMIC and the Diana logo are
trademarks of Bloomsbury Publishing Plc

First published in Great Britain 2019
Paperback edition published 2020

Copyright © Isabelle Torrance, 2019

Isabelle Torrance has asserted her right under the Copyright, Designs
and Patents Act, 1988, to be identified as Author of this work.

For legal purposes the Preface on p. x constitutes an extension of
this copyright page.

Cover design: Terry Woodley
Cover image: Attic chalice krater depicting Iphigenia and satyrs,
380 bce. DEA / A. DAGLI ORTI

All rights reserved. No part of this publication may be reproduced or transmitted
in any form or by any means, electronic or mechanical, including photocopying,
recording, or any information storage or retrieval system, without prior permission
in writing from the publishers.

Bloomsbury Publishing Plc does not have any control over, or responsibility for,
any third-party websites referred to or in this book. All internet addresses
given in this book were correct at the time of going to press. The author and
publisher regret any inconvenience caused if addresses have changed or sites
have ceased to exist, but can accept no responsibility for any such changes.

A catalogue record for this book is available from the British Library.

Library of Congress Cataloging-in-Publication Data
Names: Torrance, Isabelle C., author.
Title: Euripides: Iphigenia among the Taurians / by Isabelle Torrance.
Other titles: Companions to Greek and Roman tragedy.
Description: London : Bloomsbury Academic, 2019. | Series: Companions to
Greek and Roman tragedy
Identifiers: LCCN 2018040891| ISBN 9781474234412 (hardback) | ISBN
9781350070073 (epub)
Subjects: LCSH: Euripides. Iphigenia in Tauris. | Euripides--Criticism and
interpretation. | Greek drama (Tragedy)--History and criticism.
Classification: LCC PA3973.I8 T67 2019 | DDC 882/.01--dc23 LC record available
at https://lccn.loc.gov/2018040891

ISBN: HB: 978-1-4742-3441-2
PB: 978-1-8496-6891-0
ePDF: 978-1-3500-7006-6
eBook: 978-1-3500-7007-3

Series: Companions to Greek and Roman Tragedy

Typeset by RefineCatch Limited, Bungay, Suffolk

To find out more about our authors and books visit www.bloomsbury.com
and sign up for our newsletters.

Pour ma marraine
Ghislaine Capron

Contents

List of Figures ix
Preface x

1 Setting, Action, Plot 1
   Date 2
   The Black Sea 4
   Action 8
   The tragic plot 26
   Conclusion 28

2 Characters and Chorus 29
   Iphigenia 31
   Orestes and Pylades 36
   Thoas 43
   Taurian Herdsman and Taurian Messenger 45
   Athena 46
   Chorus 47
   Conclusion 55

3 Ethnicity and Gender 57
   Taurians and Greeks 59
   Male and female roles 68
   Conclusion 77

4 Ritual and the Gods 79
   Human sacrifice, Artemis and Iphigenia 82
   Halai and Brauron 85
   Choes 90
   Divine design and rational intellect 92
   Conclusion 98

5	Reception	99
	Inter-ethnic relations	99
	Gender dynamics	109
	Religion	117
	Conclusion	121

Glossary of Greek and Technical Terms	123
Guide to Further Reading	125
Selected Chronology	127
Notes	129
Bibliography	147
Index	161

Figures

1.1	The World of Iphigenia	5
1.2	Campanian red-figure krater, 330–320 BCE, Louvre K404	20
1.3	Apulian red-figure hydria, 370–360 BCE. Museo Archeologico Nazionale, Naples	21
2.1	Roman fresco from the House of L. Caecilius Iucundus at Pompeii, c. 10 BCE	48
5.1	Illustration for Goethe's *Iphigenie auf Tauris*. Engraving after a drawing by Ferdinand Rothbart (1823–1899)	104
5.2	Roman sarcophagus, c. 140 CE, Glyptothek, Munich, Germany	118

Preface

It has been very enjoyable to return to this play, which was the focus of my PhD thesis, completed in 2004 under the supervision of Judith Mossman at Trinity College Dublin. I owe Judith a significant debt of gratitude for her patience, generosity and encouragement during my formative undergraduate and postgraduate years at TCD. My views on Euripides' *Iphigenia among the Taurians* have not changed significantly since I defended my PhD, and much of the content of this volume is derived from that earlier work. At the same time, my understanding of the play has been enriched (and occasionally challenged) by the important scholarship that has appeared in the past fifteen years, to which I draw attention in the Guide to Further Reading. The final version of this book has benefited also from the comments of an anonymous reviewer on an earlier draft.

A Marie Curie co-fund research fellowship at the Aarhus Institute of Advanced Studies, Aarhus University, in Denmark, has afforded me the opportunity to write this book and the Institute has also covered the costs associated with reproducing images and compiling the index. It is a great pleasure to acknowledge that support. I am thankful too for the expert editorial advice of Alice Wright and Emma Payne at Bloomsbury Academic, and for the series editor Tom Harrison's kind invitation to produce this particular volume. The book is dedicated to my godmother, Ghislaine Capron, who, like Iphigenia, values ancient Greece, enjoys dramatic intrigues, and has travelled to far-flung locations.

1

Setting, Action, Plot

Iphigenia among the Taurians is one of our most exciting surviving dramas from antiquity. It tells the tale of a young princess whose father had lured her to his army's encampment under the false pretext of marriage to Greece's most eligible bachelor, the warrior hero Achilles. When she arrives for her wedding, however, she discovers that it had been a ruse to cover her father's true intention of offering her as a human sacrifice to Artemis in order to secure victory for his military campaign against Troy. That part of the story was dramatized *in extenso* by Euripides in his later play *Iphigenia at Aulis* (produced posthumously in 405 BCE), but *Iphigenia among the Taurians* is set after the sacrifice, and after Iphigenia's father, Agamemnon, has met his own doom, murdered by his wife Clytemnestra after returning victorious from the bitter ten-year-long Trojan War. The sacrifice of Iphigenia had been a crucial motivation for Clytemnestra's act of homicide in the *Agamemnon* of Aeschylus. This murder, in turn, generates the pressure on Iphigenia's brother Orestes to commit matricide in order to avenge his father's death. He is subsequently pursued by his mother's Furies (spirits of vengeance) and must seek purification. The saga of cyclical vengeance was well known, not least from the famous *Oresteia* trilogy of Aeschylus, first produced in 458 BCE. Imagine, then, the thrill of discovering that Iphigenia is not dead, but was saved by Artemis at the moment of her death, unbeknownst to the Greeks, and was established as priestess in a cult of human sacrifice (and of Greek men, specifically), in a far-flung corner of the Black Sea! This is the premise of *Iphigenia among the Taurians*, which presents a forlorn but highly intelligent heroine exiled from home and trapped in the service of a barbarous ritual overseen by a barbarian community. Just as all hope seems lost for Iphigenia, Orestes and his best friend Pylades turn up on these foreign shores on a mission for Apollo to steal the statue of Artemis from her temple and return it to Greece. The dramatic tension reaches fever pitch as Iphigenia prepares to sacrifice her brother, without realizing who he is. The relief that comes from their eventual recognition is short-lived, however, as the daring escape plan hatched by Iphigenia seems close to being discovered at every turn. Even as the trio make it back to the Greek ship, the sea is against them and recapture seems certain. Only at the final moment does the goddess Athena appear to ensure their safe departure.

This was one of Aristotle's favourite plots because it is exquisitely crafted and exhilarating to the last, a point to which we shall return. It features a terrifying set representing evidence of human sacrifice, novel props, such as Iphigenia's letter and the portable statue of Artemis, beautiful songs, and innovative theatrical scenes like the ritual procession for the purification ceremony at sea. Its cast of characters, ranging from a feisty priestess and her mentally ill but valiant brother to an enigmatic barbarian king, is both engaging and intriguing (Ch. 2). In addition to its capacity for generating exciting theatre, however, the play also asks pointed questions about social roles and inter-ethnic relationships (Ch. 3), and about theological and philosophical issues (Ch. 4). Moreover, the rich reception history of *Iphigenia among the Taurians* has only recently received the attention it deserves (Ch. 5).

Date

Iphigenia among the Taurians was produced towards the end of the fifth century BCE, around 414. Greek tragedy, which originated in the late sixth century BCE and had developed rapidly in the fifth century, was by now a well-established art form. Euripides himself, the younger contemporary of Sophocles, had been producing tragedies for at least forty years since his first attested production in 455 BCE, the lost tragedy *Daughters of Pelias*. These tragedies were performed at the City Dionysia, an annual Athenian festival held in honour of Dionysus. The religious and ritual aspects of this festival will be addressed in Chapter 4. For now, we observe that Euripides would have produced three tragedies and a satyr drama for each festival in which he competed, and would have been judged against two other competing playwrights. We do not know which other plays were produced with *Iphigenia among the Taurians*. The structure of the plot – a gutsy heroine trapped in a barbaric land, who hatches an escape plan with the help of a would-be male rescuer – is similar to Euripides' *Helen*, and to his lost *Andromeda*. These similarities led Matthew Wright to argue that the plays were performed as a trilogy in 412 BCE (the date securely attested for *Helen* and *Andromeda*), and that our only surviving satyr drama, *Cyclops* (normally dated to *c.* 408 BCE), was the accompanying satyr play.[1] The arguments put forward by Wright regarding the engagement of all these plays with issues of mythology, identity, illusion and fifth century BCE intellectualism are intriguing. However, most scholars have preferred to estimate a date for *Iphigenia among the Taurians* that is separate from these other dramas.

Euripides is known to have loosened the metrical structure of the spoken parts of his tragedies over the course of his career. Dialogue and spoken sections of Greek tragedy were normally rendered in iambic trimetres. An iambic foot (or unit) is made up of a short syllable followed by a long syllable ($\cup$ —), and an iambic metron is composed of a pair of these units ($\times$ — $\cup$ —), where × (called 'anceps') stands for a syllable that can be either long or short. The iambic trimetre, as the name suggests, is comprised of three iambic metra in sequence: × — $\cup$ — | × — $\cup$ — | × — $\cup$ -. The pattern is identified by

Aristotle as most closely resembling ordinary speech (*Poetics* 1449a21–8, *Rhetoric* 1404a31–5).[2] Later Euripidean plays contain much higher numbers of resolved feet, meaning that a syllable that should normally be long has been replaced with two short syllables. This development in Euripides' style has enabled reasonably secure conjectural dating of his plays based on the metrical patterns therein, and the proposed production date of 414 for *Iphigenia among the Taurians* has been estimated on these grounds.[3]

The Black Sea

Iphigenia among the Taurians is set in the land of the Taurians, as we are told in the customary Euripidean prologue speech outlining the background of the plot (1–66, at 30). The Taurians were an ancient tribe who lived on the northern coast of the Black Sea in southern Crimea around ancient Chersonesos, or the Tauric Chersonese (see Fig. 1.1). The fifth-century BCE ethnographer Herodotus (4.103) records some of their customs, including their practice of sacrificing shipwrecked sailors and stray Greeks, providing the earliest references to this tribe along with Euripides' play. Historically, the Greeks had established several colonies on the Black Sea coast from at least the sixth century BCE. Athens had important trade relations with Greek settlements in the Black Sea and exerted significant influence in the area during the fifth century BCE. Plutarch reports in his *Life of Pericles* (20), that the Athenian general Pericles sailed around the Black Sea in a display of might, probably around 436/7 BCE.[4] With the outbreak of the Peloponnesian War between Athens and Sparta in 431, the Black Sea colonies, who were unaffected by the war, became an increasingly valuable source of revenue and food supply for Athens. A production date of 414 BCE for *Iphigenia among the Taurians* coincides with a point at which Athenian influence in the region was

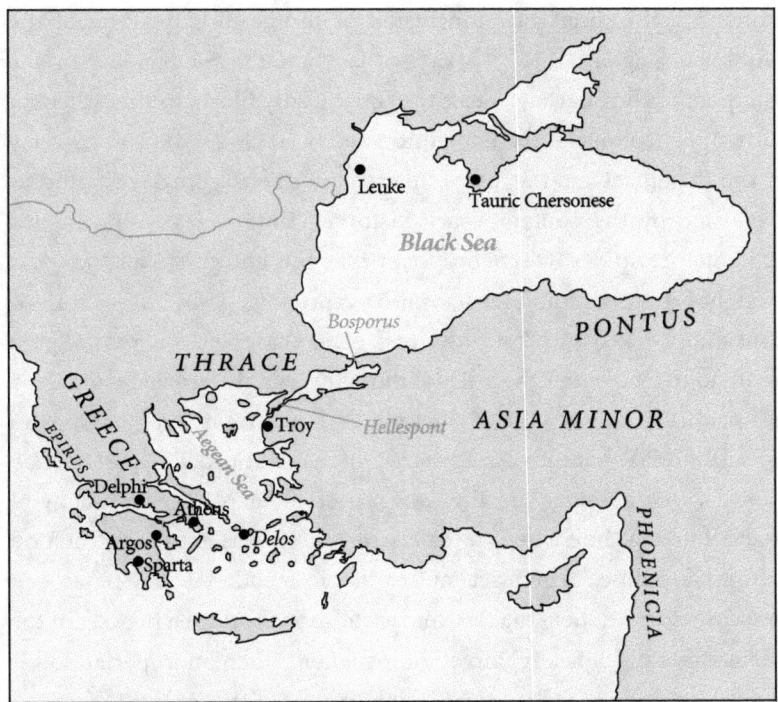

Figure 1.1 The world of Iphigenia.

going into decline due to Athenian military losses in the on-going Peloponnesian War (431–404 BCE).

Euripides' other plays from this period muse on the causes and consequences of war. *Trojan Women*, produced in 415 BCE, depicts the sufferings of the captive women of a sacked city. The tragedy would have been striking in the context of the recent sack by the Athenians, in 416 BCE, of the island of Melos, a Spartan ally that had attempted to remain neutral during the Peloponnesian War. The negative representation of the Greeks in *Trojan Women*, and of the violence of war, casts an implicitly critical light on the actions of the Athenians at Melos.[5] *Helen* was produced in 412 BCE, the year following the disastrous conclusion of the naval expedition of the Athenians against Sicily (413 BCE), when the Sicilians, with the support of the Spartans, dealt the final deadly blows to the Athenian attempt at conquest. The expedition had been clouded in controversy from the outset and the losses suffered by Athens were devastating, as reported by the contemporary historian Thucydides (6–7). In this climate, Euripides' *Helen* proposes that the entire Trojan War was fought for a phantom Helen, sent by capricious gods. The victorious but shipwrecked and destitute Greek general Menelaus lands in Egypt only to discover that the wife he thought he had retrieved from Troy was actually in Egypt the whole time, and the woman on his ship is an insubstantial phantom. As Barbara Goff has noticed, Euripides' *Helen* and *Iphigenia among the Taurians* repeatedly exploit terminology of salvation at a time when the safety of Athens was extremely high on the city's political, rhetorical and strategic agenda.[6] It may have been no coincidence, then, that Euripides chose to produce a play set in the dangerous Black Sea region at a time when Athenian imperial power was declining and Athens was losing control of that area.

The reputation of the Black Sea as a dangerous place came about, in large part, because it was notoriously difficult to navigate. Strong currents were easily exacerbated by prevailing winds, and its open expanse offered few favourable points of anchorage.[7] It was commonly and euphemistically known in classical Greece as the Euxenos Pontos 'Hospitable Sea', a technique of positive appellation designed to appease powerful negative forces. Another example would be identifying the Erinyes (Furies) as Eumenides (Kindly Ones). The name Axenos Pontos 'Inhospitable Sea' is associated by the Greek geographer Strabo (7.3.6) with savage natives who inhabited the coastal areas before the foundation of the Greek colonies, although Herodotus attests that such natives still existed in the fifth century.[8] Nevertheless, it is a mythological and pre-colonial world that Euripides seeks to evoke in his play, a fact emphasized by the insistent identification of the sea, and indeed the land, as exclusively *axenos* 'inhospitable' (94, 124–5, 218, 253, 341, 395, 438, 1388). The voyage from Greece to the land of the Taurians, undertaken by Orestes and Pylades at Apollo's command, is marked as an arduous quest, with parts of the journey referred to by the Chorus (393–4, 422–6, 435–8). The men sailed through the channel from the Propontis (Sea of Marmara), through the straits of the Bosporus, past the mythical 'Clashing Rocks', and into the Black Sea. They then turned northwards along the coast of Thrace and passed by the island of Leuke (now called Snake Island) on their course.[9] Adverse currents will prevent their escape homeward at the end of the play (1394–7), until Athena intervenes to ask Poseidon to calm the seas.

The action of the drama is set in front of a temple of Artemis at the shoreline (cf. 1196) on a raised outcrop of rock (cf. 1429–30). Of the two long side-entrances characteristic of the open-air Greek theatre, one side leads to a space further along the coast, where Orestes and Pylades have hidden their ship; the other leads to the Taurian city. The temple seems to have provided visual evidence for the practice of human sacrifice performed there through representations of severed human heads or skulls in place of animal skulls, with human blood staining both the columns and the altar in front of the temple (72–3, 404–6). This would tally, in a general sense, with Herodotus' description of the Taurian practice of decapitating enemies and displaying the severed heads above their houses as apotropaic forces (4.103).[10] Evidence of human sacrifice would have adorned the otherwise recognizable backdrop of a Doric-style Greek temple, whose features are observed by Orestes and Pylades on their arrival. It has 'high encircling walls' (96–7), and its doors have 'bronze-wrought bolts' (99). The façade is decorated with triglyphs (113) and the columns are topped with gilded coping stones (128–9). The temple must have been a visual feast of bronze, gold and red. A number of other tragedies by Euripides are set in front of temples. *Suppliant Women* is set at the temple of Demeter and Kore (Persephone) at Eleusis, and *Children of Heracles* is set at the temple of Zeus Agoraios at Marathon. Only in *Ion*, however, do we get a description of the temple as we do in *Iphigenia among the Taurians*. The temple of Apollo in *Ion* (1612–13), however, features a door-knocker in contrast to the bronze-wrought bolts of the Taurian temple. Such door-knockers could be clung to by suppliants seeking asylum (e.g. Hdt. 6.91). In *Ion*, the Athenian queen Creusa clings the temple door-knocker in gratitude for the positive resolution of the drama's events. The absence of such a knocker on the Taurian temple thus casts it, like the land, as an inhospitable location.

Action

Iphigenia's prologue speech (1–66)

Iphigenia enters from the temple, carrying the Z-shaped temple key that distinguishes her as its priestess (cf. 131), and which commonly appears on vase-paintings (as on the cover image of this book).[11] The opening prologue is marked by a strong sense of Iphigenia's isolation. This is conveyed through the account of her genealogy and betrayal by the Greeks (1–27), but also through her office as priestess in an abhorrent cult of human sacrifice (28–41).[12] The fact that she lives in the temple (65–6), which would have been exceptional for a priest or priestess under normal circumstances, further emphasizes her isolation and her bond with the goddess Artemis who, as is usual in Greek thought, inhabits the temple through her cult statue.[13] Iphigenia will later articulate her desperate isolation when she laments that she is 'without marriage, without child, without city, and without friend' (220). The first part of Iphigenia's speech also generates a tension that continues throughout the play. Iphigenia is both a victim (if survivor) of human sacrifice, which the 'civilized' Greeks condoned and believed was successful, and the overseer of 'barbaric' rites of human sacrifice practised by a 'savage' tribe (see Ch. 2).

The dramatic motivation for Iphigenia's appearance is her desire to relate a disturbing dream she had, which she has interpreted as signalling the death of her brother Orestes. Before she goes back into the temple to retrieve implements for making libations in her brother's memory, Iphigenia mentions her servants, Greek women, who for some reason have not yet arrived (64–5). This leads us to expect the entry of the Chorus, but surprise entries are a favourite technique of Euripides, and it is not the Chorus who arrive but Orestes and Pylades.[14] The suspense surrounding their furtive arrival is thus heightened by the possibility that the men might be apprehended at any moment by the Chorus. Iphigenia bolts the temple doors firmly behind her, leaving Orestes and Pylades to consider forcing or engineering an entrance (99–101) before abandoning the idea.

Arrival of Orestes and Pylades (67–122)

Orestes and Pylades arrive from the shore (67). Both are armed with swords that they will later use to defend themselves against the Taurians (323, cf. 296). The unannounced and unexpected appearance of Orestes, who believes his sister Iphigenia is dead, at the very moment when Iphigenia has announced her conclusion that Orestes is dead, is a masterstroke of dramatic irony. The danger of the situation is emphasized by the urgency of the dialogue between Orestes and Pylades, which opens with a pair of lines that are rhymed and matched exactly in phrasing (67–8).[15] They survey the ominous surroundings and we learn that Orestes has been sent to the land on Apollo's orders to retrieve the statue of his sister Artemis from the temple. Having concluded that there is no reasonable way into the temple, they decide to hide in a cave on the shore and return to their task under cover of night.

Opening song (123–235)

The Chorus members in *Iphigenia among the Taurians* represent the Greek female temple attendants of Iphigenia. They enter from one side-entrance, the town, as Orestes and Pylades leave by the other, which leads to the shore. They arrive in response to a summons from Iphigenia (137–8), which must have been sent outside dramatic time before the opening of the play. The Chorus members take their places in the orchestra (the dancing space in front of the stage building) as they sing their opening song (*parodos*). The *parodos* in this play is a duet between the Chorus and the distressed heroine, who reappears soon after the Chorus's arrival. Iphigenia returns from the temple with attendants (143), one of whom carries a gold vessel which holds the libation for Hades (167–9). At 169 the vessel is handed over to Iphigenia at her command. She begins her prayer and pours the libation for Orestes. The exchange between Iphigenia and the Chorus during the *parodos* emphasizes their parallel situations as Greek women trapped in religious service in a foreign land. The lyric metres of this song express heavy mourning.[16]

Taurian Herdsman reports capture of Greeks (236–391)

A Taurian Herdsman enters, announced by the Chorus (236–7). He is the first non-Greek character we meet. He may have worn a distinctive cap and trousers associated with non-Greeks. Vase paintings, such as the illustration on the cover of this book, show Thoas or his attendants wearing this garb, but no attention is drawn to his costume, nor indeed to Thoas's costume, in the text of the play. He announces the capture of two Greeks on the shore, who are to be prepared for sacrifice. The *stichomythia* (line-by-line exchange) between the Herdsman and Iphigenia (246–55) accelerate the pace and entice us into the Herdsman's vivid narrative of Orestes' fit of madness and subsequent capture (260–349).¹⁷ Iphigenia responds with resignation: 'Very well then' (342). She sends the Herdsman on his way to bring the men to the temple (342–3). Her dream, and her contingent belief that Orestes is dead, has steeled her more than usual to the task of presiding over the sacrifice of her next victims (348–50).

Chorus sing about the arrival of the Greeks (392–455)

The song considers the dangerous voyage from Greece to the inhospitable land of the Taurians and the grisly local practices. The first *stasimon* (a choral ode subsequent to the *parodos*) is made up of four stanzas, in two responding (strophic) pairs. The dominant metre of the song is aeolo-choriambic, a distinctive rhythm used by the lyric poets of the eastern Aegean such as Sappho, Alcaeus, and Anacreon. Its basic metrical pattern is — ∪∪ — ∪ —. It recurs at 1089–152 and in 1234–83, leading Parker to call this 'the thematic rhythm' of *Iphigenia among the Taurians*.¹⁸ Since this metre is associated with a geographical location rather than with a specific emotion, it may have helped to convey the sense that the Greeks are trapped in the east. It seems most likely that Iphigenia remains on stage while the Chorus sing and dance their first *stasimon*. It is not unusual for a character to be present during a choral song in Greek tragedy, and there is no indication in the text that Iphigenia goes back into the temple to re-emerge later.¹⁹

Build-up to the recognition (456–826)

The entrance of Orestes and Pylades is announced by the Chorus in chanted anapaests (456–66). This metre was used to announce slower entries, such as funeral processions or persons condemned to death (as here).²⁰ No longer armed, the men appear as prisoners in bonds (456–7), and are escorted by Taurian guards. Iphigenia repeats her previous expression of resignation, 'Very well, then' (467, cf. 342), as she begins preparations for the sacrificial ritual. The repetition highlights the burden Iphigenia bears, trapped in her role as officiating priestess in these gruesome sacrifices. Nevertheless, she is clearly in control of the stage action, and the Taurian guards obey her orders to untie the hands of Orestes and Pylades, and to go into the temple and prepare what is needed (468–71). Iphigenia's own attendants will be sent into the temple at 724.[21] Iphigenia will then finally be alone with Orestes and Pylades, and the sympathetic Greek Chorus, providing the dramatic opportunity for recognition and conspiracy scenes. In the build-up to recognition scene, it is crucial for the dramatic tension that Iphigenia does not recognize the name 'Pylades', which had been given to her by the Herdsman (249). Nevertheless, having ascertained that the pair are from her hometown, they strike a deal: she will spare one of them if he brings a letter back to Argos for her. Having agreed on this plan, Iphigenia leaves the stage to retrieve her letter.

Iphigenia goes into the temple (642), while her attendants guard Orestes and Pylades (636–8). This gives the men a chance to discuss Iphigenia in her absence, to wonder who she is, and to ask why she is so concerned about the Argive royal family (657–71). They argue over who should be the one to bring the priestess's letter back to Argos, with each man proposing to die so that the other can be saved. Orestes convinces Pylades that he should go back to Argos. Since Pylades is married to Orestes' sister Electra, their progeny will ensure the survival of the ancestral line (672–724). This decision generates the horrifying scenario that Orestes will be sacrificed by his own sister, unbeknownst to all parties. The atrocity, although ultimately avoided, is sufficiently heinous to generate in an audience the fear required by Aristotle's theory of tragedy put forward in his *Poetics*, to which we will return below.

Iphigenia returns from the temple with her letter (724). She orders her attendants to go into the temple to make preparations for the sacrifice (725–6), and the scene is now set to allow for a recognition sequence. The 'letter' is, strictly speaking, an ancient Greek writing tablet made of wood. Several 'pages' could be tied together through holes made in the wood. Hence Iphigenia's letter is described in a poetic periphrasis as having 'many-leaved folds' (727). Wooden tablets could be inscribed directly with a sharp instrument. Aristophanes' *Women at the Thesmophoria* (765–84) contains a parody of such writing where a character tries to inscribe wooden oars with a message. Alternatively, the tablets could be covered in wax for a message to be inscribed before the wax had set. Such tablets could then also be reused.[22] For dramatic purposes, it does not matter whether or not Iphigenia's 'letter' has been inscribed directly or through the medium of wax. In fact, we discover that Iphigenia has not written the letter herself. Rather it was written for her by a Greek captive condemned to be sacrificed, who had pitied her and judged her not guilty for her part in the sacrifice (584–7). In this sense, Iphigenia differs from Phaedra in Euripides' *Hippolytus* who does write her own letter. When Iphigenia later decides to reveal the contents of the letter, there is no indication that she reads the letter aloud rather than summarizing what it says (761). This contrast between Iphigenia and Phaedra underlines the differences in their success at controlling their relative scripts, where writing functions as a metaphor for plot construction. The literate Phaedra is entirely successful in causing the destruction of her stepson Hippolytus. In fact, Phaedra's letter has been analysed as a type of curse tablet.[23] Iphigenia, on the other hand, will ultimately fail in her aim to get back to her familial home in Argos since she will be consigned to the service of Artemis at Brauron in perpetuity (1462–7).[24]

The letter is a remarkable and novel prop, seemingly introduced to Greek tragedy by Euripides. Only tragedies by Euripides featured letters on stage, as far as we can tell. Letters appear in his *Hippolytus*, *Iphigenia among the Taurians* and *Iphigenia at Aulis*, as well as in the fragmentary dramas *Hippolytus Veiled*, *Palamedes* and *Stheneboea*.²⁵ In *Iphigenia among the Taurians*, the letter holds a unique dramatic function in precipitating the recognition scene and features on vase paintings related to the play (Iphigenia hands the letter to a seated Pylades on the cover of this book). It also supersedes traditional recognition tokens as a physical marker of proof. Confirmation of Orestes' identity is conveyed, after the contents of the letter have been revealed, only through knowledge of family artifacts rather than through their physical presence. The recognition scene is delayed, however, first by Iphigenia's demand of an oath from Pylades (735–52), and secondly by the repeated interruptions to Iphigenia's explanation of the letter (772, 777, 780). Ironically, Iphigenia's insistence on reciting the full contents of the letter further delay the recognition once Orestes has realized the truth (777). When her report is finally complete, Pylades can immediately fulfil his oath by taking the letter and handing it over to Orestes (791–2). Orestes discards the prop (793) and rushes to embrace his sister (795–7), but Iphigenia, who has not yet recognized Orestes, pulls away in horror. He catches her robes but falls short of a proper embrace (798–9). Iphigenia's reaction is appropriate to her position as a priestess, and is parallelled by other Euripidean heroines who are appalled by the advances of unrecognized male kin. Electra initially rejects Orestes in *Electra* (223), and Helen reprimands Menelaus in *Helen* (567). Iphigenia requires proof of Orestes' identity before accepting his claim (808).

Surviving Greek tragedies include no fewer than four plays in which Orestes is reunited with a long-lost sister. Only in *Iphigenia among the Taurians* is that sister Iphigenia, but the three other tragedies that feature recognition scenes between Orestes and Electra are significant for appreciating the novel way in which the scene between Iphigenia and Orestes has been handled. In Aeschylus's *Libation Bearers* (168–235), Orestes is recognized by a lock of his hair and a footprint found by Electra as she pours lustral water (129) on

Agamemnon's tomb, and by a piece of weaving that Electra had given him as an infant. In Sophocles' *Electra* (1222–3), Orestes is recognized by a signet ring that had been his father's. Euripides' *Electra* (513–44), meanwhile, makes reference to a footprint and a lock of hair at Agamemnon's tomb, and to the possible existence of a piece of weaving. These tokens are rejected by Electra, however, and Orestes is eventually recognized through a scar on his forehead (*El.* 573–5). In each case, it is a physical token that convinces the sister of her brother's identity. Euripides plays with the Aeschylean model in his *Electra*, and he does so again, though in a different way, in *Iphigenia among the Taurians*.[26] Orestes offers Iphigenia four pieces of private information related to family crimes as a means of proving his identity, rather than any physical proof. The first three pieces of information evoke the Aeschylean recognition tokens in a general sense (weaving, lustral water and a lock of hair). Orestes has heard from Electra that there was a quarrel between his ancestors Atreus and Thyestes (over a golden lamb, described in the *parodos* 189–202), and that Iphigenia had long ago created a fine piece of weaving depicting the sun reversing its course in response to that quarrel (811–17). He then reminds Iphigenia of the lustral water that accompanied her to Aulis, and the lock of hair she sent back to her mother, intended marriage tokens that became instead mementoes of death (818–21). For good measure, Orestes adds information of which he has personal visual knowledge. This is important because, in Greek tragedy, reports based on autopsy are deemed more reliable than those based on hearsay.[27] The spear with which their ancestor Pelops killed Oenomaeus, thus winning the hand of Oenomaeus's daughter Hippodamia, is hidden in the maidens' quarters of the palace (822–6). The detail seems to have been invented by Euripides, and the location of the spear in the maidens' quarters, rather than elsewhere in the house, is strange.[28] The reference brings us back to Iphigenia's opening lines which recounted her genealogy and woes beginning with 'Pelops, son of Tantalus' (1).

Together, the informational proofs revisit three generations of family crimes. Pelops traditionally kills Oenomaeus and wins Hippodamia through ill-omened treachery and sabotage.[29] The quarrel between Atreus and Thyestes would eventually lead to adultery (Thyestes sleeping with Atreus's wife), murder, and cannibalism (Atreus butchers Thyestes' children and feeds them to him, referenced in Aeschylus's *Agamemnon* 1217–22). Thyestes' surviving son Aegisthus will assist in the murder of Atreus's son Agamemnon, who, of course, is responsible for sacrificing Iphigenia after succumbing to a mental state described in Aeschylus as 'impious, impure, unholy' (*Ag.* 219–20). Unlike the other recognition scenes, then, the reunion between Iphigenia and Orestes is marked by the emotional weight of ancestral crimes that bind the family together, crimes that continue with Orestes' matricide.

Reunion duet (827–99)

After hearing Orestes' proofs, Iphigenia relents and embraces him as she sings (827–8). The recognition duet is a genre that belongs to later tragedy. Such duets gave the male actors who played female roles the chance to perform a song in lyric metres while a male character responded in the iambic trimetres used in tragedy to represent ordinary speech, and we shall return to gender dynamics more fully in Chapter 2. The division of roles ensures the dominant voice of the heroine in the duet. The song is delivered by Iphigenia primarily in the dochmiac metre, which expresses a heightened sense of emotion, often distress. Here, Iphigenia's joy is mitigated by a heavy focus on her previous betrayal and suffering (853–64) before she turns her attention to planning an escape (865–99). In the first part of the song, Iphigenia's dochmiacs are interspersed with iambic trimetres, some of which contain striking runs of short syllables conveying rising levels of excitement.[30]

Conspiracy scene (900–1088)

The recognition gives way to further questions from Iphigenia concerning her family and other Greeks. Electra, Orestes tells her, is married to Pylades who stands beside him. It is notable that, after a brief comment following the reunion of the siblings (902–8), Pylades makes no spoken contribution for the remainder of the scene nor, indeed, for the rest of the play. Where Pylades' role as Orestes' companion, and protector, had been significant in the first part of the play, focus now shifts onto the relationship of the siblings. Orestes and Iphigenia both refer to Pylades in the third person using deictic pronouns (915, 916, 917, 918, 920), and this has the effect of excluding him from their personal exchange. It may also be worth noting that Pylades becomes a mute character at the same point in the play that his counterpart in Aeschylus famously spoke brief but momentous lines, being otherwise a mute character in that tragedy (*Libation Bearers*, 900–2).[31] In a play where Aeschylus's *Oresteia* trilogy is consistently evoked, this may not be a coincidence.

After hearing of Orestes' matricide, Iphigenia decides to exploit the crime in order to convince the Taurian king that the victims must be washed in the sea for purification. She will also claim that they have touched the goddess's statue and that it too must be purified. This should enable all three to get back to Orestes' ship with the statue and make their escape. Iphigenia then considers that she will need the assistance of the Chorus for the plan to succeed (1052). She appeals to the Chorus members to keep silent about the plan and supplicates them in turn in a formal fashion: 'I beseech you by your right hand, and you, and you, and you by your dear cheek, and by your knees and by those dearest to you at home' (1068–70). Supplication of this kind was common in Greek culture. It could be effected figuratively or through physical contact. Since Greek tragedy tends to draw attention to the movements of its characters, it seems reasonable to conclude that

Iphigenia supplicates the Chorus physically in the manner she describes.³² She kneels into a suppliant position and clasps the hands and knees of a representative number of Chorus members who are close by. She reaches up to touch the cheek of one Chorus member. The well-known supplication of Zeus by Thetis in *Iliad* 1 (500–2) is similar. Thetis crouches down, touches Zeus's knees, and stretches up her hand to Zeus's chin. The supplication of multiple persons in turn, however, is a unique scene in surviving Greek tragedy, although it is not uncommon for characters to throw themselves to the ground. In fact, such theatricality is favoured by Euripides.³³ Iphigenia rises again at the Chorus's positive response to her plea (1075). The Chorus members were in any case well-disposed to Iphigenia, but the supplication generates a binding agreement that they will keep her secrets. The Chorus members effectively offer Iphigenia an oath of loyalty, by calling on Zeus as witness to their complicity (1077). Later in the play, they will prove that loyalty by deliberately misleading the Taurians and intervening in the action in a manner most unusual for a Greek Chorus. Having secured the assistance of the Chorus, Iphigenia urgently sends Orestes and Pylades into the temple (for the king is on his way) and follows them after a brief prayer to Artemis (1079–88). This leaves the Chorus alone for their next singing and dancing performance.

Chorus lament for their lost homeland (1089–1152)

The second *stasimon* of the Chorus is made up of four stanzas (strophes), in two pairs. The first two stanzas (strophe a, and its responding antistrophe a), and the final stanza (antistrophe b) muse on the pain of having been forced the leave Greece and the hope of one day returning. The third stanza (strophe b) contrasts Iphigenia's imminent escape back to Greece with the disheartening fact that the Chorus will be left behind. The dominant metre of the song, as at 392–455, is aeolo-choriambic.³⁴

Deception scene (1153–1233)

The Taurian king, Thoas, enters with his attendants, from the town. His arrival is not announced, and he confronts the Chorus directly with questions about Iphigenia and the captives. No attention is drawn to his costume in the text, but he will probably have worn the distinctive trousers and cap typical of foreigners in Greek art with a symbol of his status as a king, such as a sceptre. Iphigenia emerges from the temple carrying the statue of Artemis, a relatively small object and an unusual prop in Greek tragedy. Statues themselves are not uncommon props, but they are normally larger free-standing objects that form part of the play's backdrop. Euripides' *Hippolytus*, for example, features statues of Artemis and Aphrodite on either side of the main entrance to the palace. Images of the statue of Artemis are common in the iconography of the play. It holds centre stage on the Athenian vase from *c.* 400 BCE that illustrates the cover of this book, while Iphigenia holds the statue cradled in her arms on a Roman sarcophagus from the second century CE (Fig. 5.2). A fourth-century BCE red-figure Campanian krater (Fig. 1.2) is unusual in depicting what appears to be a life-size statue of Artemis on a pedestal in barbarian dress (and holding a bow).[35] Artemis also features in iconography as a divinity in Greek dress seated by the Taurian temple above the human characters, as in Fig. 1.3.

Thoas expresses his shock at Iphigenia's removal of the statue from its base in the temple, and an exchange follows between the two in *stichomythia* (1159–1202). The heightened pace of this type of dramatic speech reflects the urgency of Iphigenia's need to convince Thoas that she must take the statue and the Greeks to a remote location on the sea-shore where she can conduct a purification ritual. Iphigenia is in control of the exchange from the beginning. As Thoas moves towards Iphigenia, she commands him not to come any closer (1159) and he does as she asks. Once Iphigenia has persuaded Thoas

Figure 1.2 Campanian red-figure krater, 330–320 BCE, Louvre K404. Iphigenia (on the right) engages in dialogue with Orestes (centre right) and Pylades (centre left) at the temple of Artemis in front of the statue of Artemis (on the left).

to agree to her plan, the tempo of the conversation increases through an exchange in *antilabai* (1203–1221) where each character speaks half a line in turn. Iphigenia asks Thoas to tie up the Greeks, and he obeys her request by sending his attendants to do so (1203–5). Throughout the sequence, Iphigenia continues making demands – the

Figure 1.3 Apulian red-figure hydria, 370–360 BCE. Museo Archeologico Nazionale, Naples, Italy. Orestes laments in the central lower space, perhaps contemplating his imminent death, as Iphigenia approaches him on the right with an attendant, and Pylades watches on confused from the left. In the upper space, Apollo (on the left) and Artemis (on the right), seated beside her temple, watch over the scene.

heads of the Greek men must be covered, some of Thoas's attendants must accompany her, others must tell the populace to remain indoors to avoid being contaminated with pollution, Thoas must go into the temple and purify it, and cover his face as the Greek men come out of the temple. Thoas acquiesces to each request. The exchange of *antilabai* concludes with a clever pre-emptive consideration proposed by Iphigenia. If she seems to be taking a long time, Thoas should not wonder about it, and he agrees that the rites of the goddess must be completed properly (1219–20). Iphigenia wishes ambiguously for the purification to turn out as she hopes, and Thoas, completely duped, unwittingly supports her prayer (1220–1).

Orestes and Pylades are now escorted out of the temple by Thoas's attendants. Their heads are covered and their hands are bound. The attendants carry with them the goddess's adornments, young lambs, glowing torches, and everything else Iphigenia needs for the purification ritual in an impressive visual display (1223–5). The adornments refer to the robes of the goddess's statue that have been removed so that the statue can be washed. The concept would have been familiar to Athenians from their annual Plynteria ('Washing') festival when the robes of the ancient statue of Athena Polias were removed and the statue washed in the sea, possibly along with the robes. The adornment of statues with robes was itself an identifiable practice in Athenian religion, occurring most ceremoniously every four years at the Greater Panathenaea festival when a new robe was presented to the statue of Athena in an important ritual.[36] Lambs are appropriate sacrificial offerings since the blood of a lamb could purify the crime of murder. Again, this type of ritual would have been familiar to Athenians. In Aeschylus's *Eumenides* (282–3), Orestes' pollution of matricide is purified with the blood of a piglet.[37] Were real lambs used in the staging? It is quite possible that they were. A lamb features as part of a preparation for a feast in Euripides' *Electra* (494–9) in a scene which also includes an unusually large number of props, and the entry song of the Chorus of satyrs in Euripides' *Cyclops* is accompanied by a flock of sheep that are driven into the 'cave' represented by the stage building. The flaming torches, designated to accompany Iphigenia's ritual, are appropriate to the worship of

Artemis, one of whose epithets is 'the torch-bearing goddess' (21). There is no reason to doubt that real flaming torches were used. In Euripides' *Helen* (865–72), the Egyptian seer Theonoe waves fiery torches around to cleanse the air, and in his *Trojan Women* (298–352) Cassandra brandishes torches in a grim parody of a marriage ritual. Other things needed for Iphigenia's ceremony might include, for example, the libation jug previously used, and a sacrificial knife for killing the lambs. These elaborate preparations ensure that the deception is entirely convincing and make for an exciting spectacle. As the Greek men and the attendants emerge from the temple, Thoas covers his head to avoid pollution. All three high-status men now have their heads covered, emphasizing Iphigenia's complete control of the situation. As she leads the procession off stage, Iphigenia prays to Artemis for success. Thoas enters the temple and bars the door behind him, while the Chorus members (and the audience) remain silently complicit in the deception.

Third *Stasimon* (1234–83) – hymn in praise of Apollo

After Iphigenia's appeal to Artemis, the Chorus sing and dance in honour of her brother Apollo, patron of Orestes, which helps to bring out the symmetry between the human and divine pairs of siblings. The short song consists of just one strophic pair, features a significant aeolo-choriambic element, and is one of Euripides' so-called 'dithyrambic' choral songs. This refers to the ornate mythological content of the song, which has been compared to the surviving dithyrambs of the poet Bacchylides. The dithyramb was a circular dance and song performed competitively by Choruses of men and boys at the same annual festival of the City Dionysia at which Athenian drama was produced.[38] The 'dithyrambic' songs are not as closely connected to the action of the play as some of the other choral songs but are nevertheless relevant to it. Here, the Chorus assert the veracity and reliability of Apollo's oracular utterances after his prophecies have been repeatedly doubted (77–81, 570–1, 711, 723). We are also given a mythological explanation for why humans are unable to interpret their dreams correctly, as Iphigenia had been unable to do at the beginning of the play.

Concluding scenes (1284–1499)

The conclusion of the short choral song coincides with the arrival of a Taurian Messenger, wearing a mask that shows him to be battered and bruised (cf. 1366). He is in a hurry to find Thoas, and the Chorus members manage to stall him for nearly twenty lines, but they fail to throw him off the scent. It is not too long before he is pounding on the temple doors and calling out to the king and his attendants to unbolt them. Thoas comes out of the temple (1311) and learns the basic facts. He announces that the fugitives will not escape his spear (1326), but then listens to the lengthy report of events from the Messenger (1327–1419). Messenger speeches are conventional in Greek tragedy, and this speech mirrors the report of the Herdsman in the first half of the play (260–339). Nevertheless, this speech is unusual in that it prevents and delays the launch of Thoas's pursuit of the Greeks and adds to the mounting tension surrounding whether or not they will be able to make their escape. The speech is also a rare example of an open-ended messenger speech in Euripides, meaning that the Messenger does not have the information with which to conclude the narrative.[39] We do not know, at the end of the speech, if the Greeks have managed to get away in the meantime. Finally, then, after a brief interjection form the Chorus, horrified that their mistress may yet be caught (1421–2), Thoas dispatches his men to hunt down the fugitives (1423–30) and tells the Chorus that they will pay later for their betrayal (1431–4).

No sooner has Thoas sent off his men, however, than Athena appears suddenly on the roof of the temple and instructs him to halt his pursuit (1435–7). She predicts the salvation of Orestes, Iphigenia, the statue of Artemis and the Chorus, all of whom will return to Greece (1442–72). Pylades receives no mention, although it is perhaps possible that his fate was addressed in the lines that are missing between 1469 and 1470.[40] Thoas immediately complies with Athena's request (1475–85). Athena commends him and announces her departure (1486–9), and the Chorus close the play with praise for Athena and for the unexpected outcome of events. Scholars disagree over whether or not the Greek theatrical stage crane (*mēchanē*) was used to effect Athena's appearance. It was commonly used to 'fly in' divine characters, but some scholars object that the crane would not be practical for such a sudden appearance.[41] On balance, it seems plausible for an appearance on the crane to remain unobserved and sudden from the perspective of the characters on stage, and it seems likely that Athena 'flies off' after announcing that she will travel to Athens with the wind (1488). The appearance of Athena, however, is unexpected also in terms of the events of the play. More likely candidates for a divine epiphany would have been Artemis or Apollo. Artemis appears at the end of Euripides' *Hippolytus* to prescribe honours for her devoted follower, and Apollo appears to close Euripides' *Orestes* as the patron of Orestes. Euripides' *Ion*, which is set at the temple of Apollo in Delphi, concludes, like *Iphigenia among the Taurians*, with the epiphany of Athena (rather than Apollo as one might have anticipated). In *Ion*, however, Athena delivers apologies on behalf of Apollo for his absence and is clearly reporting Apollo's message directly (1555–70). This is not the case in *Iphigenia among the Taurians*, although both plays share some important Athenian concerns, which helps to explain Athena's appearance. The identity of Ion as the true-born son of the ostensibly childless Athenian queen, and his ability to continue the Athenian royal line, are central to the plot of *Ion*. Meanwhile, *Iphigenia among the Taurians* contains mythological explanations (aetiologies) for three different Attic cults, more aetiologies than any other surviving tragedy (see Chapter 4). In light of the connections that this play draws between Orestes, Iphigenia and Attica, then, it makes thematic sense for Athena to close the action, though the absence of Artemis or Apollo remains noticeable.

The tragic plot

For a modern audience, it would seem strange to call *Iphigenia among the Taurians* a tragedy. All disasters are averted in the end, the 'barbarians' follow divine orders to give up their cult of human sacrifice, and all the Greeks are ceremoniously repatriated. Yet Aristotle referred to this play in his *Poetics* as an example of the best kind of tragic plot (1454a4–7), along with Sophocles' *Oedipus the King* (1453a7–10). He also stated that Euripides is the most tragic of the dramatic poets (1453a12–15, 1453a25–30). The identification of *Iphigenia among the Taurians* along with *Oedipus the King* as examples of the best kind of tragic plots is surprising for a modern reader, who will see the two plays as very different. Both dramas, however, include a powerful reversal of fortune (*peripeteia*) and a recognition (*anagnōrisis*), where characters undergo a change from ignorance to knowledge, two elements which Aristotle considers crucial to the construction of an effective tragic plot. The term used by Aristotle to capture the concept of a reversal dependent on *peripeteia* and *anagnōrisis* is *metabolē* (*Poetics* 1452a23, 1452a31), the same term that appears in *Iphigenia among the Taurians* to mark the hope that Orestes may yet survive after Pylades has agreed to bring Iphigenia's letter back to Argos. Urging Orestes not to despair, Pylades stresses that 'extreme ill-fortune at times gives way to extreme reversals (*metabolas*)' (721–2). Moreover, Euripides exploits the term *metabolē* in several dramas to draw attention to the plot construction.[42] This pattern of reversal, then, which must happen in a plausible manner, as through the letter device in *Iphigenia among the Taurians*, seems to be tragedy's defining element for Aristotle, rather than an emphasis on some ultimate evil.[43] Aristotle also makes the point that the pleasure derived from the 'disaster-averted' type of plot is more characteristic of comedy (1453a35–9), which must be why this plot type, including extended mistaken identities followed by recognition scenes, became popular in Hellenistic and Roman comedy. The plot of Plautus's *The Captives*, for example, bears more than a passing resemblance to *Iphigenia among the Taurians* in presenting a pair of male friends in difficulty, with one about to become a victim (a prisoner of war in this case) to an unsuspecting relative (his father).[44] Moreover, the adventure and rescue plot of *Iphigenia among the Taurians* would become a staple of various subsequent genres from the ancient Greek novel to Hollywood movies, as Edith Hall has documented.[45]

There remain quite a number of surviving Greek tragedies, however, that end in resolution rather than disaster. Aeschylus's *Eumenides* is one example, but the plot type seems to be most frequent in Euripides. Catastrophes are either entirely or partly avoided in the conclusions of his *Alcestis*, *Andromache*, *Helen*, *Ion* and *Orestes*.[46] This has led modern scholars to categorize such plays in a variety of ways. *Iphigenia among the Taurians* has been called a 'tragicomedy', a 'melodrama', a 'romance' or a 'romantic comedy', a 'proto-comedy', a 'non-serious' drama, and a play with qualities of satyr drama.[47] Most recently, it has been termed a 'pre-romance', or a *Tyche* play (i.e. a play determined by luck).[48] This scholarly obsession with determining the genre of *Iphigenia among the Taurians* is rooted in the simple fact that modern audiences expect a tragedy to end in disaster whereas ancient audiences did not. As a way of bridging the impasse between ancient and modern understanding of tragedy, several contemporary scholars have demonstrated that *Iphigenia among the Taurians* is properly tragic within fifth-century BCE expectations, that the play addresses serious issues, or that the ostensible 'happy ending' is in some ways superficial, leaving the audience with a disturbing message at the play's conclusion. Elizabeth Belfiore, for example, observed that, 'on an Aristotelian reading ... the *IT* is a better-constructed, more serious, and more "tragic" play than modern scholars often believe'.[49] David Sansone underlined the serious thematic motif of sacrifice running through the drama, while Matthew Wright has argued that *Iphigenia among the Taurians* exposes the tragic limits of human knowledge and a dispiriting lack of connection between appearance and reality.[50] More generally, Justina Gregory and Donald Mastronarde have both stressed the complexities and nuances of the Greek tragic genre.[51] As we will see in the next chapter, the conclusion of *Iphigenia among the Taurians* may not even be as satisfactory for its protagonists as it at first appears.

Conclusion

This exciting drama, much-loved in antiquity and thereafter, draws its longevity from its meticulous structure, from the exhilarating pace of its action, and from its setting which explores a world in which familiar Greek norms are pushed to unexpected extremes. The combination of the Black Sea location, a cult of human sacrifice, the reunion of long-lost siblings, and a cliff-hanger escape plot have secured the place of *Iphigenia among the Taurians* as one of antiquity's most influential texts. As we turn now, in the next chapter, to the representation of the characters and the Chorus, we will trace the ways in which Euripides' play creates uniquely engaging personae.

2

Characters and Chorus

All actors and Chorus performers in Greek tragedy were male, a fact that can be difficult to remember given the large number of female roles and female Choruses in surviving dramas. Another feature of Greek tragedy, which can seem alien to a modern audience, is the prominent role of the Chorus itself, a group made up, by Euripides' day, of fifteen performers trained to sing and dance in unison. Choral odes can seem on the surface to be irrelevant to the dramatic action. It is important to consider, however, that tragedy itself developed from choral song and dance, when one performer broke off from the main group to act out one or more different roles. Aeschylus was credited with introducing a second actor, and Sophocles a third, and all surviving Greek tragedy is composed for performance by a maximum of three actors with speaking parts. The choral odes of Greek tragedy, then, are fundamental to its structure and to the development of its themes, while the actors often played more than one role. The proliferation of actors' roles and the presentation of female characters played by men were facilitated by the use of masks that covered the whole head of the actor, with appropriate wigs attached. In *Iphigenia among the Taurians*, the distribution of parts could easily have been the following. A protagonist played Iphigenia and Athena, a deuteragonist played Orestes and Thoas, and a tritagonist played Pylades, the Taurian Herdsman, and the Taurian Messenger. Although Orestes appears on stage at the end of Iphigenia's exchange with Thoas, he has no speaking part in the scene, which leaves the actor who played Orestes free to become Thoas while a mute extra dons Orestes' costume.[1] These issues of performance raise interesting questions about how male actors trained to sing and act differently for male and female roles. Although we know very little about the training of ancient actors, we do know that they were highly skilled.[2] It may also have been the case that the distinctive voice of an actor could be used to create connections between different roles.[3] When the actor playing Iphigenia took on the role of Athena, this may well have cemented the sense of conflation between the mortal Iphigenia and a divine goddess that is suggested in the play (on which see Chapter 4). Similarly, if the actor who played Orestes takes over as Thoas, the destabilizing of ethnic stereotypes, discussed in Chapter 3, may have been felt more acutely.

Certainly, the cast of characters in *Iphigenia among the Taurians* is extraordinary and unusual for several reasons. Iphigenia is the only example of a priestess in the main role of a surviving tragedy, which makes her remarkable and gives her a level of legitimate authority that is unmatched in any other tragic heroine from antiquity. At the same time, the play also stresses her extraordinary personal grief at being cheated out of her marriage and forced into exile providing unexpectedly profound psychological insights into her suffering. Orestes is depicted paradoxically both as a successful quest hero and as a figure plagued with mental illness, while his companion Pylades has a more important role in this drama than he does in other Greek tragedies, specifically as the person who cares for Orestes when he is suffering. In fact, the devotion of each friend to the other is one of the most significant strands in the reception history of the play (see Chapter 5). Thoas remains an enigma of sorts since we learn nothing about his person, ancestry, family or history. Is he a savage brute or is he simply a pious Taurian? Piety is a significant concern for all three Taurian characters (Thoas, the Herdsman and the Messenger), but it is the appearance of Athena that establishes new and appropriate religious rituals. The Greek Chorus members too are pious in their devotion to Artemis's priestess, but as a group they interfere directly in the action to a degree that is unparallelled in Greek tragedy. They lie openly to the Taurians thereby also putting their own lives on the line, and the audience is left concerned for the fate of all the Greeks until Athena's miraculous epiphany.

Iphigenia

We noted in the previous chapter how Iphigenia controls the male characters on stage, particularly in the second half of the play. This authority comes from her identity as a priestess, which is one the defining aspects of her character, and is linked with her isolation. In Chapter 3, we will discuss the importance of female priesthoods in classical Greece and, in Chapter 4, we will address the relationship between Iphigenia and Artemis in the context of Greek religion. A further important characteristic in Iphigenia's identity is her status as a figure of failed normative transitions. Her transition to marriage fails when the prospective marriage to Achilles becomes her own sacrificial death. The conflation of Iphigenia's marriage and death would become a significant theme in Euripides' later *Iphigenia at Aulis*.[4] In *Iphigenia among the Taurians*, however, Iphigenia's survival and existence in the land of the Taurians also mark her failed transition to death. All the Greeks believe she is dead (8, 176–7, 563–4, 831), even though she is still alive. At the end of the play, Iphigenia will be fated to remain in the service of Artemis at Brauron, outside of Athens, receiving offerings after her death belonging to women who have died in childbirth (1464–7). Such women would also have been considered figures of failed transitions in Greek culture, since they had failed to complete the transition to motherhood by their untimely deaths. The drama's conclusion, then, ties Iphigenia in perpetuity with symbols of failed female transitions, just as she herself 'remains permanently arrested in a liminal phase'.[5]

Iphigenia is very much preoccupied with her failed transition to marriage. Her opening speech briefly recounts her lineage (1–5). However, a far longer proportion of the speech is devoted to how and why she was brought to Aulis on the pretext of marriage to Achilles, but was actually to be slaughtered like an animal (6–29). Accounts of, and references to, Iphigenia's sufferings are repeated throughout the play (209–17, 337–9, 354–77, 538–9, 565–6, 770–1, 784–6, 818–21, 853–67, 920, 1082–4, 1418–19, cf. 1113, 1187). Details of the ordeal emphasize the conspiracy of the Greeks and the personal betrayal of Iphigenia. Agamemnon wanted the crown of victory over Troy (12) and revenge for his brother Menelaus, whose wife Helen had been stolen from him (13–14). Calchas, the army's prophet, reminds Agamemnon that he had vowed to sacrifice to Artemis the finest thing the year would bear and names Iphigenia as that finest thing, whose sacrifice, he claims, is needed to gain fair winds to Troy (15–24). Odysseus takes her from her mother on the pretext of marriage (24–5). Instead, she is lifted high over the sacrificial altar to be killed with a sword (26–7). Artemis saves her and substitutes a deer, unbeknownst to all (28–9). Iphigenia laments: 'they took me to the sands of Aulis, alas, an ill-wedded bride' (215–16), emphasizing the conspiracy of the group of Greek men who betrayed her. She ends up 'without marriage, without child, without city, without friend, who was wooed by all the Greeks' (220, 208). She is not able to participate in the festival of Hera, patron of married women (221), nor is she able to weave the robe (*peplos*) for Athena (222–4) and participate in the festival of the Panathenaea. The language of music sets up a contrast between the destiny Iphigenia had wished for herself working on the 'sweet-voiced loom' (222) and the reality of her grim predicament inflicting 'a bloody and unmelodious fate on strangers' (225–6). She had begged her father many times to spare her life, that she was losing shamefully at his hands, while her mother was singing wedding hymns for her in ignorance back in Argos (364–71). Instead, Iphigenia's father becomes the priest at her sacrifice (360).

It is noteworthy that Iphigenia does not willingly accept her death in *Iphigenia among the Taurians*. In this sense she is more like the Iphigenia of Aeschylus's *Agamemnon* (228–47), who protests her sacrifice, than like the Iphigenia of Euripides' later *Iphigenia at Aulis* who ultimately embraces death. In fact, voluntary sacrifice is the norm in Euripides. The title character in *Alcestis*, Polyxena in *Hecuba*, Macaria in *Children of Heracles*, Evadne in *Suppliant Women*, one of the daughters in the fragmentary *Erechtheus*, and Menoeceus in *Phoenician Women* all go willingly to their deaths.[6] In *Iphigenia among the Taurians*, however, Iphigenia insists that she was an unwilling victim. In Greek cultural terms, this means that the sacrifice is ill-omened since animal sacrifice, on which Iphigenia's sacrifice is modelled, requires a symbolic nod of consent from the victim. In Aeschylus's *Agamemnon*, the ill-omened sacrifice of Iphigenia signals future suffering for Agamemnon and his own death at the hands of his wife Clytemnestra. Here too, it is briefly reported that Agamemnon has been killed by Clytemnestra (552).

What is most extraordinary, however, about Euripides' presentation of Iphigenia in *Iphigenia among the Taurians* is the degree of psychological insight into her suffering. This is generated, in large part, through the remarkable plot. Iphigenia has *both* experienced the betrayal and terror of being sacrificed like an animal by her own father *and* has miraculously survived to tell the tale. She is thus able to articulate in detail what is only hinted at in Aeschylus's version, and Euripides capitalizes on this by showing that Iphigenia is unable to forget the horrors of that day (361). Moreover, the lure of marriage to Achilles was a cruel trick (371, 539, 857) and Iphigenia dwells insistently on the trauma of the deception. Although Iphigenia has been saved from death by Artemis, the focus on her failed transition to marriage highlights her personal grief at having been robbed of the normative transition for a young Greek princess. As the end of the play makes clear, Iphigenia will never marry and will never return home to Argos as she had wished (774–6, cf. 175, 221, 515, 639–42, 750–2). This means that, although Iphigenia is reunited with her brother, escapes from the land of the Taurians, and gets back to Greece, she will never have the life she had wanted. Iphigenia and Orestes are not present when Athena predicts their fates, so we do not know their responses. However, the emphasis Iphigenia places on her unhappily unmarried state and on her desire to get back to Argos, means that the drama's conclusion is not as 'happy' for Iphigenia as it might first appear.[7]

The imagery used to describe Iphigenia's future is significant. She will remain in the service of Artemis 'in the holy meadows of Brauron' (1462–3). Locating an unmarried woman in a meadow in Greek myth often prefigures her abduction and rape by a male figure. The most important example of this phenomenon is the rape of Persephone, who is abducted from a meadow while picking flowers by her uncle Hades and is brought down to the Underworld, as recounted at the opening of the *Homeric Hymn to Demeter*. In Euripides' *Ion* (887–96), Creusa reports that she was abducted and raped by Apollo as she had been picking flowers in a meadow. Europa was also traditionally abducted by Zeus from a meadow while picking flowers.[8] Meanwhile, Herodotus (4.145) identifies Brauron itself as the location of the abduction of Athenian women by Pelasgians. As Helene Foley notes in her commentary on the *Homeric Hymn to Demeter*, the 'motif of abduction from a meadow ... suggests the girl's readiness for marriage'.[9] In Euripides' later *Iphigenia at Aulis* (1545), the transmitted text locates Iphigenia's sacrifice in the meadow of Artemis at Aulis thus developing the play's conflation of marriage and sacrificial death. By identifying the meadows of Brauron as the location for Iphigenia's service and final resting place in *Iphigenia among the Taurians*, Euripides emphasizes her tragic entrapment in a permanent state of readiness for marriage, initiated at Aulis before the Trojan War, all while she is forever to be denied that transition.

It is a further deep irony of Iphigenia's fate that she has ended up presiding over the kind of human sacrifice to which she was subjected by the Greeks. It might be argued that there is a certain poetic justice to Iphigenia's role in overseeing the sacrifices of shipwrecked Greek men, after a group of Greek men seeking to set sail had condemned her to a sacrificial death. In fact, the Taurian Herdsman suggests as much to Iphigenia regarding Orestes and Pylades whose sacrifices, he proposes, might make amends for her own sacrifice at Aulis (336–9). But Iphigenia does not see things that way. She is grieved at her bloody task and describes the piteous cries and piteous tears of her victims (227–8). She has always been gentle and compassionate towards her victims (344–5). Iphigenia's anger is directed primarily at those she deems responsible for her misery, specifically Helen and Menelaus who might be made to pay if they turned up on the Taurian shores (354–60). The Chorus later repeat the hope that Helen might be killed by Iphigenia at the Taurian temple and pay the penalty for her offences (439–45). Iphigenia also claims to have been hardened by the dream that she believes indicates Orestes' death (348–50). Like many victims of parental child abuse, however, Iphigenia voices equivocal sentiments about her abusive parent, in this case her father. She repeatedly identifies her father as the perpetrator of her sacrifice (8, 211, 360–8, 565, 784, 854, 920, 1083), and calls her fate 'unfatherly' (863), but she also expresses sadness at the news of his death (553), calls him wretched like herself (565), and renounces any anger towards him (991–2). Notably, in the moment of leaving aside her anger in order to focus on saving her brother, Iphigenia refers to 'the man who killed me' and does not use the word 'father' as elsewhere. This distancing effect allows Iphigenia to move forward with a renewed hope of returning home with her brother. The final third of the play underlines Iphigenia's intelligence as she successfully puts in motion her plan to escape with Orestes, Pylades and the statue of Artemis. The control she wields over the male characters is also part of this drama's exploration of gender relations, which will be addressed in Chapter 3.

Orestes and Pylades

The Orestes of Greek tragedy is always a troubled figure and is often accompanied and assisted by his best friend Pylades. After following the instructions of Apollo to kill his mother, Orestes is hounded by her Furies. In Aeschylus's *Oresteia* trilogy, Orestes is purified of blood pollution through the sacrifice of a piglet (*Eum.* 282–3) but must then stand trial for matricide at the homicide court in Athens. He is acquitted by Athena's vote in his favour. Euripides acknowledges this trial in *Iphigenia among the Taurians* (939–78) but insists that some of the Furies remained unpersuaded by Athena and continue to pursue Orestes. For that reason, Apollo has sent Orestes on a quest to steal the statue of Artemis from the Taurian temple and bring it back to Athens, the implication being that this will finally dispel the Furies. This challenge casts Orestes in the mould of a heroic figure, who must undergo an arduous journey to a dangerous place, face the possibility of death, and retrieve a precious object. The narrative pattern resembles those of Heracles who must steal the apples from the garden of the Hesperides, or bring the three-headed dog Cerberus back from Hades, or of Jason who must steal the golden fleece from Colchis and who, like Orestes, must rely on the assistance of a female (in Jason's case that person is Medea). The fact that the quest precipitates the reunion of Orestes with his sister, who is assumed dead, can also be compared to narratives of a hero's encounter with dead relatives in the Underworld such as Orpheus's attempt to retrieve his wife from Hades or Odysseus's confrontation with ghosts from his past in *Odyssey* 11. Karelisa Hartigan has called Orestes' quest his *katabasis*, a word meaning 'descent' that refers to a heroic journey to Hades and back.[10] There are certainly katabatic elements in Orestes' experience. The land of the Taurians functions as a 'land of the dead' for Greek sailors, and Iphigenia is a 'ghost' from Orestes' past. Iphigenia may also be symbolically associated with Hecate, the goddess of crossroads, including the threshold between life and death. Earlier Greek poetry by Hesiod and Stesichorus links Iphigenia to Hecate, and Iphigenia's patron Artemis is suggestively called 'torch-bearing' (21), a more common epithet of Hecate.[11] Most significant, however, is the passage of Orestes' ship through the 'Clashing Rocks' (241, 260, 354–6, 422, 746, 889–91, 1389) since these represent the gates to the Underworld through which a hero must pass.[12] We noticed in Chapter 1 that the Black Sea is repeatedly referred to as 'the inhospitable sea' in this play, and the dangerous nature of the voyage is further emphasized by the Chorus. They wonder how Orestes and Pylades managed to pass through the Clashing Rocks, the shores of Phineus (a blind prophet persecuted by the Harpies ('Snatchers'), who snatched his food before he could eat it), and the white shores (i.e. the island Leuke) where Achilles is located after his death (422–8, cf. Fig. 2.1). Clearly, this wonder signals the accomplishment of a significant feat.

Orestes himself, of course, is not a typical quest hero since he is subject to hallucinations in which he sees his mother's Furies, and he must rely extensively on Pylades for assistance (285–314). This is noteworthy in the context of Greek tragedy since Pylades elsewhere plays a very minor role in events. In Aeschylus's *Libation Bearers* (900–902), Pylades speaks three important lines but is otherwise a mute character and he does not appear in Aeschylus's *Eumenides*. In the *Electra* plays of Sophocles and Euripides, Pylades is a non-speaking extra. Only in Euripides' later *Orestes* (of 408 BCE), which also deals with Orestes' madness, does Pylades have a significant role in the second half of the play. In *Iphigenia among the Taurians*, imagery of twisting and circling is emblematic of Orestes' madness. The Furies have driven him to complete 'many twisting courses' (81) and he seeks an end to his 'wheel-borne madness' (82). The metaphors are derived from chariot-racing, thus conflating a noble and heroic pursuit with the affliction of madness. Later in the play, the metaphor returns when Orestes reports that the Furies drove the bloody bit into his mouth (935), as if he were the horse and the Furies his charioteer. This pattern of both suggesting and undermining Orestes' heroic status is repeated throughout the play, while Pylades, who is untainted by madness must repeatedly come to Orestes' aid. From his first arrival on stage at the temple of Artemis, Orestes is anxious. Worried that someone may apprehend them, Pylades must reassure Orestes that he is keeping a good lookout (62–3). Orestes then asks Pylades a series of questions concerning the location, and it is Pylades who provides all the answers and undertakes a thorough inspection of the premises (69–76). As Orestes concludes the account of his sufferings, he once again turns to Pylades for advice, asking a series of questions about what they should do, and concluding, before Pylades can answer, that they should simply go back to the ship and flee (95–103). Again, Pylades takes control of the situation, pointing out that fleeing would go against their custom and would dishonour Apollo's oracular instruction (104–5). He comes up with a plan to hide and return by night to complete their mission under the cover of darkness (106–12), and concludes by saying: 'Noble men endure ordeals, while cowards are worth nothing anywhere' (114–15). Orestes agrees, but has shown himself to be weak-willed and thoroughly dependent on Pylades in his opening scene.

If Pylades is responsible for the planning of the theft, he is also responsible for the physical protection and care of Orestes during his fit of madness on the Taurian shore. The Taurian Herdsman relates how the two young men were spotted and were thought to be divine by a god-fearing cowherd, perhaps Castor and Polydeuces or sons of one of the Nereid sea nymphs (267–74). Another man, however, ridicules this proposition and declares them to be shipwrecked sailors who should be captured as victims for Artemis, and most of the herdsmen agree (275–80). As we shall see in Chapter 4, the tension between traditional belief in anthropomorphic gods and rationalized rejection of such is an important theme in the play. In fact, Orestes and Pylades are not shipwrecked sailors, and while they are not gods either, their comparison to divinities fits the heroic model of epic where humans with divine patrons appear to be as gods. So Odysseus is made to look divine and awe-inspiring by Athena in his encounter with the princess Nausicaa on the Phaeacian shore, and again in front of his son Telemachus in Ithaca (*Od.* 6.243, 16.183). At the end of the Herdsman's report, it is made clear that Orestes and Pylades are divinely protected since they remain miraculously untouched by the shower of stones that is pelted at them (328–9), though the source of that divine protection is never identified. In the report of Orestes' madness, the epic model is thus once again both developed and undermined. Madness is an affliction suffered only by humans and not by gods who are rather the cause of Greek tragic madness.[13] At the same time, the Herdsman's narrative suggests that Orestes has heroic and noble characteristics.

Orestes' seizure on the shore is so severe that the herdsmen hide and fear that Orestes might die (295–6). He shakes his head back and forth, groans loudly, with hands trembling, wandering madly, shouting like a hunter as he hallucinates. He sees Furies threatening to kill him, their snakes breathing out fire and gore, while they flap their wings. One Fury holds his dead mother in her arms, a burden of stone, ready to be thrown at him (282–90). This terrifying sight causes him to consider how he might flee (291), which had also been his proposition when faced with the horrific temple and its altar drenched in human blood. This time, however, unprompted by Pylades, Orestes decides to stand and fight. Sword in hand, he leaps into the middle of the cattle (believing that they are the Furies) 'like a lion' (296). This brief simile is important because it is frequently used of Homeric warriors to describe an attack comparable to that of a ferocious predatory animal.[14] Elsewhere in tragedy, where Orestes and Pylades have committed murder, they are 'twin lions' (Aeschylus, *Libation Bearers* 938; Euripides' *Orestes* 1402–3, 1555). We can also compare Euripides' Heracles, driven mad by the goddess Hera, who attacks and kills his wife and children while hallucinating that they are his enemies. His mood is like that of a wild lion (*Her.* 1211), as he becomes like the very beast he had previously subdued (*Her.* 360, 466, 579, 1271). The description of Orestes leaping 'like a lion' as he slaughters the herd of cattle in *Iphigenia among the Taurians* thus evokes Homeric heroism, savagery and madness all at the same time. Of course, the fact that Orestes' victims are not powerful enemies but defenceless animals emphasizes the depth of his delusion. In this sense, he is most similar to the hero Ajax who, as reported in Sophocles *Ajax* (41–73), was driven mad by Athena and slaughtered cattle and sheep in the mistaken belief that he was killing the Greek enemies who had dishonoured him. In Orestes' case, after he has killed the cattle, we are told that 'the expanse of the sea bloomed blood-red' (300). This image also contains significant epic and tragic resonances. The pleonasm 'expanse of the sea' is derived from epic language, while the metaphor of the sea blooming with corpses had been exploited by Aeschylus (*Ag.* 659) to described the Greeks drowned in storms on their return from Troy.[15] The cumulative effect of these evocative details is to stress the extent of Orestes' madness, and how it prevents him from functioning properly within the epic mould.

Orestes and Pylades are recognized by the Herdsman as formidable fighters of noble stock, who might only be subdued by a large number of armed but inferior Taurians (302–5). The word used by the Herdsman to describe the pair as noble is *eutrapheis* (304). This literally means 'well-bred' or 'well-reared', which in the case of Orestes is problematic given his crime of matricide. Again, we see in the details given by the Herdsman that although Orestes is ostensibly of noble birth, he has been debilitated as a result of his actions. The question of correlation between lineage and 'noble character' is a theme explored by Euripides more fully in his *Electra* (e.g. 366–400, 550–2), where both Orestes and the Old Man doubt the connection between birth and good character. Events in *Electra* confirm that low status characters behave more nobly than those of royal ancestry.[16] In *Iphigenia among the Taurians*, it is Pylades who exhibits noble behaviour as Orestes collapses foaming at the mouth (307–8), a symptom of Greek tragic madness.[17] Pylades protects his friend, wipes away the foam and shields Orestes with his cloak amidst the hail of assaults from the Taurians who seize their chance to attack when Orestes has fallen (308–14). Pylades demonstrates his true friendship by putting the needs of Orestes above his own, conforming to Aristotle's definition of a friend as someone who tries to accomplish for his friend's sake what is good for the friend (*Rhetoric* 1361b36-7).[18] Orestes will also prove to be a good friend to Pylades when he insists on being the one to face death so that Pylades can go back to Greece with Iphigenia's letter and return to his wife Electra (688–707). Orestes rejects Pylades' proposal that they should die together, persuading him that his survival will benefit Orestes' own family line by securing its future through Pylades' offspring with Electra (Orestes' sister). In this way, Pylades can agree to save himself while also acting in the interests of Orestes. He remains a true friend according to Greek ethics of friendship where the combination of altruism and self-interest was important.[19] Later antiquity found the relationship between Orestes and Pylades depicted in *Iphigenia among the Taurians* to be a philosophically inspiring example of ideal male friendship (see Chapter 5).

During the earlier attack by the Taurians, Orestes had also embraced death. Suddenly regaining his faculties during the onslaught, he had leapt up and realized that he and Pylades were surrounded and vastly outnumbered. According to the Herdsman's report, Orestes then made a 'terrifying' speech: 'Pylades! We are about to die! We must make sure that we die in the noblest way! Draw your sword and follow me!' (320-2). The Taurians retreat to the rocky gullies where they continue pelting the pair with stones. They surround the Greeks and eventually subdue them (323-33). It is made clear, however, that Orestes and Pylades are captured only with great difficulty, and because the large number of Taurians manages to exhaust them. The narrative thus concludes by emphasizing the valiant and heroic qualities of Orestes and Pylades. Orestes leads the pair, but we know from the earlier scene in front of the temple that Orestes' courage has been rekindled by Pylades and his dependence on Pylades has been further confirmed by the Herdsman's report. After the recognition scene, however, as we saw in the previous chapter, Orestes becomes dependent on Iphigenia and Pylades' role becomes essentially defunct.

Before the recognition scene, Orestes had refused to give Iphigenia his name for fear of being mocked (502), in a manner typical of tragic heroes for whom being the object of mockery was unendurable.[20] In the report of their attempted escape, however, Orestes proudly identifies himself to the Taurians by his name and lineage (1358-63), but before the Greeks can sail away, Poseidon, patron of Troy and opponent of the descendants of Pelops, pushes the Greek ship back to shore (1389, 1414-17). The sequence of events is reminiscent of Odysseus's encounter with the Cyclops, Polyphemus, where he withholds his name, claiming instead that he is called 'No one'. Odysseus manages to escape death and get back to his ship, but boasts his true name to the Cyclops as his ship is leaving the shore (*Od.* 9.502-5). This enables Polyphemus to call down the curse of Poseidon on Odysseus, which causes Odysseus much trouble at sea (*Od.* 9.528-35). It is evident in the *Odyssey* that Odysseus's boast was foolish, but he manages to escape from the land of the Cyclopes. In *Iphigenia among the Taurians*, Orestes will not be able to escape without the intervention of Athena (also Odysseus's patron), even though he manages to fight off the Taurians and get Iphigenia safely onto the ship (1354–85). Overall, then, the narrative echo conforms to the pattern evident throughout the play of implicitly comparing Orestes to heroes from epic while simultaneously stressing his inability to fulfil that role as a result of his crimes.

Thoas

It is late in the play when we actually meet Thoas (1152), but he is mentioned early on in Iphigenia's prologue speech. 'Thoas rules the land, a barbarian among barbarians, who, by running with a swift foot equal to wings, got his name on account of his swift-footedness' (31–3). Thoas's name suggests the Greek word for 'swift' (*thoos*), and the name occurs in different mythological contexts. One of the kings of the island of Lemnos, for example, was reputedly called Thoas, and a joke is made about him in the comedy *Women of Lemnos* by Aristophanes. A fragment from this lost play (fr. 373) reads that Thoas was the slowest of men at running, implying that he was inappropriately named. We will discuss in Chapter 3 how the issue of 'barbarism' is played out in *Iphigenia among the Taurians*. For now, however, we should notice that Iphigenia's description of Thoas as 'swift-footed' evokes the common epithet of Achilles, whom Iphigenia had expected to marry and who is, according to the Chorus, on the white shore's fine-coursed running tracks (436–7), on the island of Leuke not terribly far away (Fig. 1.1). What is also interesting, is that, unlike the Egyptian Theoclymenus in *Helen*, Thoas does not desire to marry the Greek princess.[21] This is quite as it should be. As a priestess of Artemis, who is patron of the unmarried, Iphigenia is not an eligible bride. We get no information on Thoas's marital situation, but no wife or children are mentioned. The association between Thoas's name and the swift-footedness regularly attributed to Achilles, who had just been mentioned (25), is thus intriguing. This could be read as an implicitly positive heroic characteristic attributed to Thoas suggesting, before we meet him, that he might be a sympathetic character.

Scholars disagree on how best to read Thoas's character. Is he a dupe and a brutish savage? Or is he a pious individual adhering to local custom in a frightening yet understandable way? My own view leans towards the latter reading, as I will explain further in Chapter 3. Perhaps most significant about the evocation of Achilles as a heroic archetype relevant to Thoas, however, are Achilles' characteristics of being straightforward rather than duplicitous and quick to anger when he has been betrayed. Thoas will display both these characteristics when we meet him. When Thoas trusts Iphigenia in the deception scene, it is because he has had no reason to doubt her to date, but when he discovers the betrayal he immediately threatens that the fugitives will not escape his spear (1326) and his anger only abates after divine intervention. As a character type, then, Thoas bears certain broad similarities to the model of Achilles.[22] This analogy, coupled with Thoas's obscure personal history, contributes to the presentation of an elusive character whose representation on stage may be open to interpretation.

It is important for the dramatic tension of the play, however, that Iphigenia's deception of Thoas should be a challenge, and this tension is generated, in part at least, I would argue, by the suggestion that Thoas has certain noble attributes and is not simply a bumbling fool. It is implied that a good relationship exists between Thoas and Iphigenia, who tells us that her devoted Greek attendants (the Chorus) were given to her as a gift by Thoas (63–4). Before the recognition scene, Iphigenia anticipates being able to persuade Thoas to allow her to send one of the captives back to Greece (741–2), again suggesting that he is a reasonable man who would be well-disposed to Iphigenia's request. As plans for open persuasion turn into a deception plot,

Thoas falls into the category of men in authority who are outwitted by women in Greek tragedy. Other examples include Clytemnestra's persuasion of Agamemnon in Aeschylus's *Agamemnon*, Helen's ability to charm Menelaus with suspicious rhetoric in Euripides' *Trojan Women*, and Medea's manipulation of Creon and Jason in Euripides' *Medea*.[23] What is most in evidence, however, during Iphigenia's deception of Thoas is his concern for proper religious behaviour. Iphigenia cleverly plays on Thoas's piety to convince him that the stain of pollution caused by the crimes of the Greeks necessitates purification rituals. He praises her conscientiousness (1202) and her concern for the community (1212), and is keen to comply when Iphigenia asks him to purify the goddess's sanctuary (1215–16). Parker observes that he 'asks shrewd and pertinent questions (1164, 1166, 1178, 1196) ... shows signs of impatience (1190, 1196) ... [and] comes dangerously close to the truth (1184)'.[24] Thoas's immediate submission to Athena in the final scenes will once again confirm his pious respect for the gods.

Taurian Herdsman and Taurian Messenger

Although they are stock characters to a great extent, the Taurian Herdsman and Messenger share with Thoas a concern for religious piety and a respect for Iphigenia as priestess. When the Herdsman reports that the two young men spotted on the beach might have been deities, the man who makes that suggestion is called 'god-fearing' (268). The man then raises his hands and prays to sea divinities (269–74), but we are told that 'another man, foolish and daring in his lack of respect for custom, laughed at the prayers', declaring the men to be shipwrecked sailors (275–7). The focalization of opinion from the Herdsman's perspective shows that his sympathies lie with the pious man.[25] The reason for which the herdsmen are at the seashore, moreover, suggests that they are conducting a ritual cleansing. When Iphigenia asks what they were doing on the shore, the Herdsman explains that they had gone there to wash their cattle in the sea (254–5). The answer apparently satisfies Iphigenia, who tells the Herdsman to continue with his report, but the audience may still wonder about this cattle-washing ritual, which appears contrived, and for which there are no known parallels. Euripides seems keen to present the Taurians as a pastoral community, and the Herdsman is the first Taurian we meet.[26] Moreover, the seashore is developed as a crucial location in this escape-drama.[27] The cattle-washing ritual allows Euripides to combine these two elements. At the same time, the scenario prefigures the deception ritual of washing the Greek men and the statue of Artemis in the escape plot, and enables a characterization of the Taurians as a pious people. The Messenger and his fellow attendants are similarly characterized by piety in their reluctance to witness the secret purification rites, even though they become concerned at the length of time that has passed and worry that Iphigenia might have fallen foul of the Greeks. It is only because of their concern for Iphigenia's safety that they finally decide to investigate (1339–44). Once the treachery of the Greeks has been discovered, the Messenger no longer trusts the Greek Chorus either, and rightly so, since they attempt to deceive him. In fact, both the Taurian Herdsman and the Taurian Messenger contribute to the drama's complex representation and manipulation of 'Greek' and 'barbarian' norms (see Chapter 3).

Athena

As a divine character, Athena gives commands and prescribes the future. The humans obey without hesitation. Appearing very briefly at the drama's close, she is aloof and inscrutable as gods are in Greek tragedy. It is clear, however, that her concerns lie with Athens, the city under her divine patronage. Artemis's sacred statue must be transported to Athens, which Athena refers to as 'my land' (1441). Instructions are given for going to 'divinely-built Athens', where a temple to Artemis should be constructed close to its outer borders (1449–51). Iphigenia must also go to the outskirts of Athens, to Brauron (1462–3), and Athena recalls that she had saved Orestes also before at the Areopagus court in Athens (1469–71). When Athena appears at the end of Euripides' *Ion*, it is also because the play's conclusion concerns Athens, in this case the acknowledgement of Ion as an Athenian prince who should now rule over Athens.

Chorus

The Chorus functions as a collective character and as an internal audience in Greek tragedy. The identity and fate of the Chorus members are connected to the main plot variously in different plays. In Euripides' *Suppliant Women* and *Bacchae*, their fate is closely tied to the action, but it has often been held that the Choruses of *Iphigenia among the Taurians* and of other Euripidean plays are irrelevant to the plot. The criticism dates back to Aristotle (*Poetics* 1456a25–7), and has been influential, though scholars have also defended the relevance of Euripides' choral odes to the dramatic action.[28] It will be argued here that the choral songs of *Iphigenia among the Taurians* develop themes of significance to the drama and that the Chorus members themselves are closely linked to Iphigenia. That close connection was, in fact, noticed and represented in antiquity on a beautiful Roman wall-painting preserved at Pompeii (Fig. 2.1).

The identity of the Chorus as Greek maidens, trapped in the land of the Taurians, in the service of Artemis clearly reflects Iphigenia's own predicament, and the connection between them is emphasized in

48　　　　　　　　*Euripides:* Iphigenia among the Taurians

Figure 2.1 Roman fresco depicting Iphigenia at the Taurian temple with her attendants; House of L. Caecilius Iucundus at Pompeii, *c.* 10 BCE.

the duet they sing as the opening song of the drama (123–235). The Chorus identify themselves as maiden servants of Iphigenia, exiles from Greece (130–6), and join her in lamenting the misfortunes of the house of Atreus (186–202). Like Iphigenia, the Chorus also regret that they are unmarried and childless (1089–97) and cannot participate in appropriate festivities (1143–52). These songs sung by maidens (*parthenoi*) evoke the Greek tradition of choral song called the *partheneia*, a type of song performed in Greek rituals related to rites of passage for young women. As Laura Swift has argued, the choral songs of *Iphigenia among the Taurians* exploit parthenaic language in order to evoke those rituals.[29] The religious identity of the Chorus as temple servants is also significant, and they are referred to as 'guardians of the temple' and 'altar-supervisors' (1284). As we saw in Chapter 1, Iphigenia does not take the Chorus members' complicity for granted and supplicates them to keep her plot secret. They agree without hesitation, but it should not go unnoticed that they are to be left behind at the mercy of the Taurians. Iphigenia promises to bring them back to Greece if she survives the voyage home herself (1067–8), but the Chorus are given no guarantees. These Greek maidens bravely put their mistress' survival above any concern for themselves. They celebrate Iphigenia's anticipated escape, while observing that she will leave them behind (1123–36), and conclude their song with a series of wishes to return home (1137–52). Those expressions of personal desire on the part of the Chorus lend depth to their collective character, and underline the sacrifice they are willing to make in order to secure the salvation of their mistress. As such, this Chorus differs significantly from the Chorus of Greek captive women in Euripides' *Helen*, who attend Helen in Egypt, and to whom the Chorus of *Iphigenia among the Taurians* is often compared (although the Chorus in *Helen* has no formal religious function). The Chorus in *Helen* (1451–1511) sing only of their mistress' escape without referencing any hope of their own for returning home. The wish that they might join the migrating cranes on their flight back to Libya contains the suggestion that they would pass over Sparta and deliver the news of Menelaus' imminent return (*Hel.* 1478–94), but they do not articulate any personal desires to return to or remain in Greece.[30] The Chorus of *Iphigenia among the Taurians*, by contrast, imagine themselves as a 'wingless bird', and so unable to escape, matching the halcyon in its song of lamentation for a husband (1089–95).³¹ They extend the dirge to reflect on their lost homeland (1096–105), and on the sorrow and suffering they endured when their city was sacked and they were sold into slavery by their enemies (1106–122). This choral song focuses primarily on the Chorus's own fate and sentiments. Out of two strophic pairs (i.e. four stanzas, 1089–152), only nine lines (1123–31) nestled in the second strophe (third stanza) are devoted to Iphigenia's escape. Within the second strophe the contrast between the two fates is emphasized by the phrasing: '*You*, mistress will be taken home by an Argive ship' (1123–4), 'but *I* will be left behind by you here' (1132–3).³² The song is thus framed by, and preoccupied with, the Chorus's personal situation of captivity and longing to return home.

The theme of travel and the desire for escape back to Greece had been significant as well in the previous choral song (392–455). There, the Chorus had wondered about the course of the journey undertaken by the Greeks to reach the Taurian shores (esp. 422–38) and had hoped someone might arrive from Greece to save them from captivity and bring them home (447–55). Both songs also emphasize the gruesome rites of human sacrifice practised in the Taurian land (402–6, 439–46, 1113–16), and pass negative judgements on the acquisition of wealth through roving and trading (407–21, 1111–12). This theme of greed for ill-gotten riches lurks in the background of the play, and is part of the ancestral history of the protagonists. In the opening song (189–201), the Chorus had reminded us of the quarrel between Atreus, grandfather of Orestes and Iphigenia, and his brother Thyestes over the golden lamb as part of the family's troubles. Although the reference is brief and the passage contains some textual problems, it is easy to recognize the myth according to which the course of the Sun was reversed, and day became night as nature reacted with horror to this quarrel.³³ The event is also referenced in the recognition scene where Iphigenia acknowledges that she wove an image of the sun's reversed course (812–17). Desire for possession of this golden fleece had led to a series of heinous crimes. Atreus had won the fleece and therefore the kingdom, but Thyestes sought revenge by having an affair with Atreus's wife, triggering the events outlined in Chapter 1.

The negative consequences of human material greed are emphasized in a more general sense by the Chorus. They are casualties of war for plunder, and have been sold into captivity 'through a trade rich in gold' (1111). Musing on the miseries of slavery does not mean that the drama has an abolitionist message. Slavery was an accepted part of life in classical Athens and throughout ancient Greece. Nevertheless, Greek tragedy is sensitive to the pathos of a fall from good fortune to misfortune. Transitioning from freedom to captivity is always lamentable in Greek tragedy, and female characters even argue occasionally that death is preferable to slavery (e.g. Andromache in Euripides' *Trojan Women*, 630–83). Since slaves were property, owning slaves was an indication of status and wealth, but the Chorus warn that it can be dangerous to seek riches. Some men become insatiable in their quest for wealth, seeking it over land and sea, and are unable to avoid excess (414–21). In the divine world, however, greed for gold is acceptable. This is part of what we learn from the Chorus's final song (1234–83), and as we shall see in Chapter 4, *Iphigenia among the Taurians* repeatedly draws contrasts between human limitations and divine omnipotence. The subject of the song is how Apollo came into possession of the Delphic oracle. As the patron of Orestes, and the god who sent him to the land of the Taurians, Apollo is intimately connected with this drama although he is absent from it.

The Chorus's song in praise of Apollo is just one strophic pair (two stanzas), but it is full of imagery pertinent to the play. According to the song, Apollo destroyed the fierce snake that guarded the oracular seat at Delphi while he was still an infant and took over the shrine, dispensing oracular truths while sitting on his golden tripod (1244–58). Earlier in the play, it had been the Fury of Orestes' mother who had been identified as a snake (236) and reference to Apollo's destruction of the snake here foreshadows his protégé's release from the Furies. The contrast between mortal and divine remains clear, however. The infant Apollo easily dispatches the snake that prevents him from achieving his goal, while Orestes suffers prolonged hounding by the Furies and requires divine aid to overcome them. Apollo too will need divine assistance from his father, Zeus, it is revealed, but he does not suffer and seems to get his way like a petulant child. We learn in the antistrophe (second stanza) that Apollo's takeover of the oracle has unseated the ancient goddess Themis (Righteousness). Themis' mother Earth is angry that her daughter has been removed from the oracular shrine and retaliates by sending humans prophetic dreams, thus making Apollo's oracle redundant (1259–69). The young Apollo then races to Olympus and pleads with Zeus to help. Zeus laughs, amused at his son's eagerness for 'gold-rich offerings' (1275), and with a shake of his hair Zeus prevents mortals from understanding their dreams thus revalidating their need for Apollo's oracular utterances (1270–83).

This explains, retrospectively, why Iphigenia misinterpreted her dream at the beginning of the play even though she had correctly understood its symbolism. She dreams that she is sleeping at home in Argos and the palace crumbles to the ground. She flees and sees just one remaining pillar of the house, which grows hair and takes on a human voice. In her dream she sprinkles this 'head' with water, in the same way she prepares victims for human sacrifice, and weeps (44–55). Iphigenia correctly understands that the pillar represents Orestes, but she mistakenly concludes that he is already dead (55–8). Dreams always turn out to be true in Greek literature, and Caroline Trieschnigg has shown how audience expectation is manipulated through Iphigenia's dream. At first, the audience will fear that Iphigenia will consecrate Orestes for sacrifice, thus unwittingly fulfilling the dream. After the recognition scene, the audience must wonder how the dream will be fulfilled since they know that it must come true, unlike the characters. Iphigenia dismisses the dream as false (569), while Orestes compares the ruinous prophecies of Apollo to flighty dreams (570–5). For the audience, however, it becomes clear that the dream is fulfilled by the purification ritual performed by Iphigenia in the sea. The final choral song confirms that dreams are truly prophetic, but by divine design, mortals are unable to interpret them.[34] It is significant that the conflict between Gaia and Apollo referenced by the Chorus was probably Euripides' own invention, while other aspects of the divine myth are known from other sources.[35] This demonstrates the thematic importance of dreams in *Iphigenia among the Taurians*, and the significance of Iphigenia's dream for creating suspense regarding the play's outcome.

The hymnal register of this final choral song provides an appropriate accompaniment to the ritual procession enacted by the Greeks as they go offstage, particularly since it had been anticipated by the Chorus that Apollo would escort Iphigenia with song on her voyage back to Greece (1128–31). William Furley comments that the Chorus in this ode 'cast a ritual veil, as it were, over the clandestine plot of the Argives'.[36] As Donald Mastronarde has noticed, the characters offstage are in a tense situation, but this tension is not carried over into the choral song, which 'provides for a stronger contrast and heightened suspense when it is reported that the escape is in jeopardy'.[37] When Iphigenia's deception is discovered, the Chorus prove their loyalty. They go further than keeping silent and actively impede the Taurian Messenger who has uncovered the escape plot. When he rushes onto the scene looking for Thoas, the Chorus first detain him with expressions of disbelief (1284–94), and then lie outright. Knowing perfectly well that Thoas is inside the temple, they tell the Messenger that they don't know where he is and they try to send him away to look for the king (1296–8). The Chorus seem to have the upper hand, but all of a sudden the Messenger exclaims that he does not believe the women (1298–90). The Chorus continue their deception calling him crazy, asking what they could possibly have to do with the escape of the Greeks, and trying to send him off in the direction of Thoas's palace (1300–1). The Messenger remains undeterred, however, and starts hammering on the door of the temple to see if Thoas is inside. When Thoas emerges and learns what has happened, it is clear that he intends to punish the Chorus women (1431–2), until Athena prevents him and arranges for the women's return to Greece praising their righteous judgement (1467–9).

Such direct choral intervention in the plot is unusual in Greek tragedy. It also seems that Euripides has gone out of his way to make the audience reflect on and pity the Chorus's plight. In *Helen*, for example, the fate of the Chorus is never addressed and no provisions are made for their return to Greece. The identity of the Chorus members in *Iphigenia among the Taurians*, as personalized (albeit collective) subjects with their own desires, has been developed to a significant extent. We have seen the degree to which they reflect on their own situation in their choral songs. Moreover, when Orestes gives Iphigenia news about her family, the Chorus burst out, interrupting the conversation, and asking emotionally: 'Oh! Oh! What about us and our parents? Are they alive? Are they dead? Who could tell us?' (576–7). Dramatically, their outburst functions as an aside, since none of the characters on stage responds and the action proceeds as if the Chorus had said nothing. What are we to make of this? To a modern sensibility, the lack of concern for the Chorus might seem callous, but it is evident that the Chorus members themselves value Iphigenia's life above their own. In a sense, the relationship between Iphigenia and the Chorus mirrors that between Iphigenia and Artemis. They are in service to Iphigenia, subordinate to her and her priestly office, and are dedicated to serving the best interests of their mistress even if it goes against their own. Similarly, Iphigenia is in service to Artemis and must proceed as the goddess wishes by presiding over the cult of human sacrifice, even if she has no desire to do so. When faced with the prospect of sacrificing new victims to the goddess, Iphigenia had addressed the Chorus claiming to have learned the following truth: the unfortunate, encountering those more fortunate, do not wish them well because of their own suffering (351–3). Yet, by their actions, the Chorus prove Iphigenia wrong in this regard since they are willing to face serious consequences in order to help their mistress escape. So Iphigenia's 'truth' is shown to be false in a play where, as Matthew Wright has demonstrated, things are rarely as they seem, beginning, of course, with the fact that Iphigenia is still alive although the Greeks believe she is dead.[38]

Conclusion

The preoccupation with the exile and entrapment of Iphigenia and the Chorus in this play is remarkable. Although Euripides' *Helen* and *Trojan Women*, produced in the same period as *Iphigenia among the Taurians*, also feature exiled or enslaved female protagonists and Choruses, Iphigenia and her attendants are unique in that they suffer no sexual advances or sexual threats. This is appropriate to their positions as servants of Artemis, but it simultaneously highlights the piety of the male Taurians who respect them. Indeed the lack of sexual content made *Iphigenia among the Taurians* a popular choice for performance in Greek at colleges in Britain and North America at the end of the nineteenth century.[39] Orestes plays second fiddle in the play, first to Pylades and then to Iphigenia, and this is also unusual for a significant male role in Greek tragedy. Orestes is defined by the pollution of matricide which undermines his abilities to function effectively. Even though he will assert himself in the end by hoisting Iphigenia and the statue of Artemis onto the ship, the escape of the Greeks will remain impeded until the intervention of Athena. These issues of inter-ethnic and gender relations that we have touched on in this chapter will now receive our full attention in the next.

3

Ethnicity and Gender

Throughout *Iphigenia among the Taurians*, Euripides evokes and manipulates expectations regarding two pairs of commonly opposed markers of identity in Greek thought: Greek and non-Greek, and male and female. Construction of identity through ethnicity and gender is, of course, common to all cultures and societies. What is interesting about Euripidean tragedy, however, is that it often raises questions about stereotypical assumptions within these broad sociocultural categories. In an important article, first published in 1984, Suzanne Saïd analysed the representation of Greeks and 'barbarians' in the tragedies of Euripides. The word 'barbarian' (*barbaros*) in Greek means 'foreigner'. The literal defining attribute of a *barbaros* is someone who speaks an unintelligible language (i.e. a language that sounds like 'bar-bar' to a Greek). The Greek word *barbaros* can be neutral in a way that the English 'barbarian' cannot. In practice, however, Greek literature could tend to associate foreigners (*barbaroi*) with non-Greek practices in a negative manner. After the Greek victories in the Persian Wars of the early fifth century BCE (490–479), for example, a contrast was drawn between 'democratic' Athenians and 'slavish' Persians in *Persians* by Aeschylus, who was a veteran of the Persian Wars.[1] As Saïd points out, however, Euripides belonged to a different generation whose intellectuals were calling into question or qualifying such distinctions. Herodotus, whose *Histories* were circulating when Euripides was a young man, gives ethnographic explanations for different customs and often posits associations or equivalences between Greeks and foreigners.[2] Contemporary philosophers, known as sophists, who were paid instructors in philosophy and rhetoric, proposed that, in their natures, all men were alike regardless of their ethnicity.[3] Similarly, the tragedies of Euripides consistently raise questions about what it means to be a 'Greek' or a 'barbarian', by representing barbaric Greeks, noble barbarians, or both.[4] In *Iphigenia among the Taurians*, Euripides implicitly asks – who are the real barbarians? The conclusion which suggests itself is that the Greeks may be more barbaric in violating their own norms than the Taurians.

When it comes to gender, the tragedies of Euripides can raise similar questions regarding stereotypes, in this case relating to traditionally male or female behaviour. It has been argued, for instance, that Medea exhibits characteristics of a male epic hero in *Medea*, and that Theseus' lyric outburst in *Hippolytus* represents an emotional struggle expressed through a normally feminine register.[5] In *Iphigenia among the Taurians*, the model of Aeschylus's *Oresteia* suggests itself. In that trilogy, Iphigenia's mother Clytemnestra rules the kingdom in the absence of her husband, a woman who plans like a man (*Ag.* 11), while her cowardly lover Aegisthus is called a woman by the Chorus of old men (*Ag.* 1625). In *Libation Bearers*, Clytemnestra calls for a traditionally male weapon, a 'man-killing axe' at the moment of her death (889), while the final play, *Eumenides*, restores patriarchal order by acquitting Orestes of matricide and sending him back to rule in Argos. Traditional gender roles are resolved also in the divine sphere, since Apollo wins out over the Furies. Athena, who is patron of both male and female spheres of activity (war and weaving), and who casts the vote of acquittal, announces that she commends the male in all respects and will not set a higher value on the life of a woman who killed her husband (*Eum.* 737–40). Euripides evokes that context in his exploration of gender roles in *Iphigenia among the Taurians*, but what is most remarkable is Iphigenia's legitimate female authority through her position as priestess which makes her unique as tragic female protagonist. Significant also is the way in which the drama stresses the value of female contributions to society, not only through ritual activity but also through childbirth, which is developed as a noticeable theme.

Taurians and Greeks

The Taurians, as we saw in Chapter 1, were a real tribe dwelling in the region now known as the Crimea. According to Herodotus (4.103), they practised the human sacrifice of shipwrecked sailors and Greeks and these sacrificial victims were offered to the goddess Iphigenia. They also decapitated their enemies and displayed the severed heads above their houses on stakes, and made a living through war and plunder. The archaeological record, however, provides evidence also for peaceful settlements in this area, and Euripides' Taurians are not as savage as he might have made them.[6] They practise human sacrifice, but the notion that this is 'un-Greek', and therefore barbaric, is undermined by the fact that Iphigenia had been sacrificed by her own father. Other wartime activities alluded to by Herodotus remain unmentioned in Euripides, and the Chorus members say that they were bought (1111–12), implying that Thoas was merely their purchaser and not their conqueror. Nevertheless, Thoas must have some military abilities. He has a cavalry and ships, and plans to kill the fugitive Greeks by throwing them off a cliff or impaling them on stakes (1421–30). In this detail, at the end of the play, we see an allusion to the kind of savagery reported by Herodotus but, from the little we can glean about Taurian life in Euripides' drama, they also seem to be a pastoral community of cattle-herders. It will be argued here that Euripides undermines and challenges a straightforwardly negative reading of the Taurians in this play, taking into account the evidence from the text and the fact that Euripides tends to represent foreigners in a sympathetic light in his dramas. It is only fair to acknowledge at this point that the play could also be performed with Thoas as a thuggish and unsophisticated brute by, for example, casting an imposing actor who can adopt threatening postures in a visibly barbarian costume and playing the deception scene to make Thoas seem like a fool. This is often how Thoas was interpreted in the play's later reception history (see Chapter 5). However, based on the text of Euripides, I believe that his Thoas and his Taurians were not presented as alienating 'others', diametrically opposed to the Greeks. Rather, they function to problematize ethnic stereotypes and to bring out the ironies of such polarities.

The Taurians, as described and represented by the Herdsman, are not warriors and are no match for the skilled Greek swordsmen whom they meet on the beach. They attack the Greeks with stones when Orestes has collapsed after his fit of madness (318–19). This may seem like an unsophisticated method of attack, but it is, in fact, the appropriate response in Greek terms to the pollution that has caused Orestes' madness. In Euripides' later *Orestes*, the title character is sentenced to death by stoning because of his pollution for matricide and the issue is central to that play.[7] Although it was very uncommon in practice, death by stoning was a recognized form of communal killing for a serious criminal in classical Athens.[8] The aim of the herdsmen is to subdue the Greeks rather than to kill them, at this point, but it remains striking that circumstances lead them to behave in a manner that is in line with identifiably Greek customs (albeit unwittingly since they have, at that moment, no knowledge of the men's crimes). In the later mirror scene, where the Taurians try to apprehend the Greek fugitives as they are escaping to their ship, they also resort to pelting the Greeks with stones after coming off the worse in a fist fight (1367–76). Meanwhile, the Greek archers on the ship keep the Taurians at bay. The detail is noteworthy because classical Greeks commonly associated archery with foreigners, and with unheroic long-distance attacks rather than heroic close combat.

Aeschylus uses the bow to represent Persians and the spear to symbolize Greeks (*Persians*, 146–9). In practice, the Greeks did rely on archers for their military exploits, but the ambivalent associations with archery persisted and were exploited by Euripides in his *Heracles*, where the title character is armed with a bow and his valour is called into question as a consequence.[9] We see, then, that ethnic stereotypes are destabilized in *Iphigenia among the Taurians* by including Greek archers and foreigners stoning a known criminal.

In the first encounter between the Taurians and the Greeks, the herdsmen use conch shells to summon help (303), and it has been suggested that this signifies their primitivism since these shells were considered to have been used before the invention of trumpets.[10] The context is important here. Trumpets were used in times of war, but conch shells remained in use among those who dwelled in the countryside for attracting the attention of neighbours.[11] The use of conch shells by the herdsmen, then, may simply reflect the pastoral nature of their occupation, rather than any ethnic stereotype.[12] Similarly, the terms used to describe the political system of the Taurians do not betray any sense of it being un-Greek. Thoas's kingly office is described with various Greek terms for king. He is repeatedly called *anax* 'lord' (63, 333, 1048, 1156, 1159, 1163, 1285, 1294, 1335, 1435), but so is Agamemnon (11, 17, 545). He is a *tyrannos* 'autocrat' (741, 1020), but the system of rule in Argos is likewise a *tyrannis* 'an autocracy' (681). He is a *basileus* 'king' (109), but so are the ancestral kings of Argos (190, cf. 670). The only term of authority used to describe Thoas alone is *koiranos* (1080, 1287), but this term has no connotations of foreignness and is used elsewhere in tragedy for Greek kings.[13] The Taurian community is repeatedly called a *polis* (the Greek term for city-state: 38, 464, 595, 878, 1209, 1212, 1214), as are the cities of the Greeks (453, 505, 1088, 1014). The inhabitants of the Taurian *polis* are 'citizens' (*politas* 1226, 1417; *astoi* 1422), like the

Greeks (495), and Iphigenia functions 'as the priestess of an imaginary polis religion'.[14] Other communities in the area, by contrast, are simply referred to as 'tribes' (890).

Herodotus (4.99–109) had identified the Taurians as one of a number of tribes who inhabit this region. Of these only the Budinians are mentioned as having a *polis* in their territory, but the inhabitants of this *polis*, the Gelonians, are descended from Greeks who had settled among the Budinians. They have temples honouring Greek gods, and speak a mixture of Scythian and Greek. Euripides' Taurians resemble Herodotus' Gelonians in that their community is a *polis* and their temple honours a Greek goddess. No ancestral connection is drawn between the Taurians and the Greeks, although the Taurians, like virtually all foreign characters in Greek tragedy, speak perfect Greek (for logistical reasons). The Phrygian slave in Euripides' *Orestes* (1366–1536), who sings in broken Greek, is the exception to the rule, but it is often through song and through music that Greek tragedy made its 'foreign' elements felt.[15] In *Iphigenia among the Taurians*, however, the Taurian characters never sing. Rather the Greek women are the ones who sing in 'foreign' tones. The Chorus respond to Iphigenia's lament by announcing that they will cry forth 'a barbarian cry of Asian songs' (179–80), in a lyric performance that must have been marked by aural features evocative of foreign music. In the report of Iphigenia's deceptive purification ritual, we are told that she 'raised the ritual cry, and began singing barbarian chants, acting like a *magos*' (1337–8). A *magos* was a type of Persian priest who interpreted dreams (Hdt. 7.37), and the word came to mean 'magician' and 'imposter' in a negative sense.[16] These connotations associated with a *magos* make it an unexpectedly appropriate comparison for a priestess who has attempted to interpret a dream and is conducting a ritually framed deception. The fact that Iphigenia is reported, by a 'barbarian', as singing 'barbarian' songs contributes to the destabilization of the Greek–barbarian dichotomy in this play.

The Taurians and their land are repeatedly designated as 'barbarian', both by the Greeks and by themselves, and there is a surface appearance of a Greek–barbarian polarity. In the deception scene, for example, Iphigenia displays a typically Greek ability in her clever manipulation of Thoas, in a sequence where Thoas finds Greece responsible for her wisdom (1180). For the classical Greeks, deception was not necessarily negative, particularly if it helped to achieve a greater good.[17] Within a creative work of poetic fiction, of course, a fictive story within the play reflects the broader structure of the whole. Iphigenia is in control of the fiction (*mythos*, cf. 1049) until the deception is uncovered, and Athena concludes the story (*mythos*, 1442).[18] It is also significant, however, that the Greeks associated the trait of honesty with foreigners. Herodotus (1.136) tells us that the Persians studied only three things until they were twenty: horsemanship, archery and honesty. The free nomadic Scythians, meanwhile, lose respect for the Ionian Greeks after being deceived by them, and in this case the guileless Scythians compare favourably to the Ionian Greeks who have been in league with the Persians (Hdt. 4.136–42). If Thoas believes Iphigenia's deception, then, it is a mark of an ethnic stereotype that need not necessarily be pejorative. We note also that Iphigenia's story is convincing because it is based, in large part, on the truth.[19] Thoas questions her extensively, from the beginning of the scene (1153–4) to the very end (1219), pressing Iphigenia to explain herself.[20] He is a rational interlocutor who asks logical questions. Iphigenia's ability to convince him, by appealing to his sense of piety, demonstrates the high degree of her intelligence.

When Iphigenia reveals that pollution has come upon the temple as a result of the crime of matricide committed by the Greeks, Thoas utters one of the most memorable lines in the play: 'Apollo! Not even among barbarians would anyone have dared that!' (1174). This horror expressed by a king who has been called 'a barbarian among barbarians' (31), and whose people practise human sacrifice, produces a deep irony. Thoas is made to invoke Apollo, unwittingly calling upon the very god who ordered the matricide. There is an ethnic association of foreignness lurking in the background here, since Herodotus (1.137) tells us that the Persians assert that no Persian man has ever killed a parent. At the same time, there is a serious point being made. If the 'barbarians' are barbaric for sacrificing Greeks, then how uncivilized are the Greeks if they can murder their own mothers? Moreover, if human sacrifice is unholy under Greek *nomos* 'law', or 'custom', as the Chorus women claim (464–7), then what kind of aberration is represented by Agamemnon's sacrifice of his daughter alluded to so often in this play?[21] By contrast, the practice of human sacrifice among the Taurians is consistently referred to as the *nomos* 'law' of the land (35, 38, 277, 586, 1189). Iphigenia even relates that the captive Greek who wrote the letter she had hoped to send home did not judge her guilty of his murder. Rather he considered that he was dying due to the local *nomos* and that the rites of the goddess were legitimate (585–7). This is significant because of the intellectual interest in the nature (*physis*) versus nurture (*nomos*) debate in contemporary fifth-century BCE Athens. Is nature or custom more significant in shaping social and political behaviour? Philosophers disagreed, and Euripides presents a range of opinions on the matter through various characters in his dramas. In support of the Protagorean understanding of the nature of man as the source of all valid conventions,[22] we can adduce the Chorus of followers of Dionysus in *Bacchae* (890–6) when they say that what is *nomimon* 'lawful' or 'customary' has its origin in nature (*physei . . . pephykos*). Theseus in *Suppliant Women* (196–213), on the other hand, argues that the natural state of humans is brutish and requires order to be imposed upon it, in line with the Atomists and Gorgias' *Palamedes*.[23] Meanwhile, a character in the lost tragedy *Aeolus*, which dealt with brother–sister incest, asks what it means for something to be shameful if it does not seem so to those who practise it (fr. 19), reflecting the view of the Athenian philosopher Archelaus that what is just or base depends not on nature but on convention.[24] In Euripides' *Andromache* (147–273), the Spartan princess Hermione attacks the Trojan Andromache's 'barbarian' nature in an attempt to degrade and dominate the slave woman who has stolen her husband's affections. As scholars have shown, however, the 'barbarian' Andromache far surpasses the Greek princess in her rhetorical abilities and in the effectiveness of her arguments.[25]

On the issue of religion, Herodotus (3.38) states that all people, without exception, believe their own customs. Greeks burn the bodies of their dead, and would never consider eating the dead bodies of their parents, whereas the reverse is true for the Callatiae tribe in India. Their custom is to eat their parents' bodies, Herodotus reports, and the tribesmen expressed great horror at the thought of burning the bodies after the Greek custom. So, Herodotus concludes, the Boeotian poet Pindar was correct when he claimed, in a poem that survives in fragmentary form, that custom (*nomos*) was 'king of all' (fr. 169a, Race 2003).[26] Euripides makes it clear that the Taurians practise human sacrifice because it is their *nomos*. Moreover, the goddess Artemis is said to delight in this *nomos* (35). The Greeks, on the other hand, have violated their own customs in horrifying ways, through crimes of filicide qua human sacrifice, and matricide. Orestes proposes violating a further Greek *nomos* when he suggests that Thoas might be killed, and Iphigenia replies that it would be a terrible thing to kill a host (1020–1). Orestes persists, suggesting that it should be risked if it can save them, but Iphigenia cannot agree although she praises Orestes' spirit (1022–3). The exchange reveals that Iphigenia considers Thoas to be her host, alluding to the Greek concept of *xenia*, which is often translated as 'guest friendship'. This convention of Greek culture refers to guest–host relationships. A guest can expect a host to provide hospitality and sustenance, while a host can expect a guest to be appreciative, well behaved, and to reciprocate hospitality in the future. In Homeric society the bond was sealed through the ritual exchange of gifts, and was hereditary.²⁷ The Trojan War, in fact, begins as a result of a breach of *xenia* when the Trojan prince Paris 'steals' the wife of his Spartan host Menelaus and escapes with her to Troy. If Iphigenia considers Thoas to be her *xenos*, as she seems to, this further enhances the positive characterization of the Taurian king, and we have noticed previously that he gave her the Chorus women as a gift.

It is significant that Iphigenia should be so concerned to avoid violating her relationship with Thoas in this way. Orestes could easily justify killing Thoas in order to save his own life without having to consider these issues. An important Roman appropriation of this myth, associated with the worship of Diana (the Roman name for Artemis), asserted that Orestes had slain Thoas. Each successive priest of Diana of the Wood, a runaway slave who was given the title 'King of the Wood', was required to slay his predecessor before taking office in emulation of Orestes.²⁸ In *Iphigenia among the Taurians*, however, by refusing to allow Orestes to kill the king, Iphigenia shows herself to be unlike her ancestors who had violated guest–host relations, often in a gruesome fashion. Tantalus, father of Pelops, first mentioned in the opening line, had abused his privilege of dining with the gods by dismembering his son in an attempt to feed the gods human flesh (386–8).²⁹ Having been reconstituted by the gods, Pelops had later killed his host Oenomaus in order to marry his daughter Hippodamia. The audience is reminded of this myth in line 2 with references to Pelops and his marriage to 'Oenomaus' daughter', and in the recognition scene when Orestes reminds Iphigenia that the spear Pelops used to kill Oenomaus was hidden in the girls' apartments at Argos (823–6). Abuse of 'hosts' turns inwards towards family members in subsequent generations. Thyestes violates his brother Atreus's marriage by sleeping with his wife, and Atreus invites Thyestes to a feast where he is fed the flesh of his own children in a quarrel that is mentioned twice (191–202, 812–13). Atreus's son Agamemnon is lured to his death in a bath on his homecoming (as dramatized so effectively in Aeschylus's *Agamemnon*).

In the land of the Taurians, there is a further irony to Iphigenia's rejection of killing her *xenos*. The word *xenos* (plural *xenoi*) means both 'host' and 'guest', but it also means 'stranger' in a more general sense. Iphigenia's office is to preside over *xenophonia* 'the murder of *xenoi*' (776) and the Greeks to be sacrificed are overwhelmingly referred to as *xenoi* 'strangers'.[30] It has been made clear, moreover, that the Greeks have landed in an *axenos* 'inhospitable' land (94) on the *axenos pontos* 'inhospitable sea' (124–5). The varied exploitation of the term *xenos* in *Iphigenia among the Taurians* allows Euripides to underline the contrast between Greek and Taurian customs. The Taurians have no concept of hospitality in the Greek sense, and this is reflected by their 'inhospitable' landscape and practices. Connecting ethnic difference with geography was common in Greek thought, and is epitomized by the Hippocratic treatise *Airs, Waters, Places* which associates biological features with climatic conditions. Herodotus, too, was 'a convinced exponent of environmental determinism'.[31] The climate of Egypt, for example, and the behaviour of the Nile river, which differs from other rivers, are linked by Herodotus to the behaviour of Egyptian people (Hdt. 2.35). What Euripides underlines, then, is that the Taurians are behaving in accordance with their own *nomoi*. The fact that they are inhospitable is very much a logical reflection of the inhospitable coastal landscape they inhabit. The Greeks, on the other hand, have repeatedly violated their own *nomoi*. When Iphigenia identifies Thoas as her host and refuses to plot his murder, she is redressing that anomaly in a positive fashion.

Helen Bacon noticed many decades ago, in her study of 'barbarians' in Greek tragedy, that Euripides is the tragedian who uses the least exotic vocabulary, elements of foreign dress, or other ethnic stereotypes, to characterize the 'barbarians' in his tragedies.[32] In *Iphigenia among the Taurians*, Euripides creates the illusion of a binary opposition between savage barbarians and civilized Greeks, and then works to undermine that dichotomy. The Greeks are cunning where the Taurians are unsuspecting, and the Taurians differ from the Greeks in their customs, but the play also makes some unsettling suggestions. Framing the Taurian practice of human sacrifice as an ethnic *nomos* emphasizes, by contrast, the aberration of the Greeks in sacrificing Iphigenia against their own *nomoi*. Furthermore, the Taurians, like the Greeks in fact, only engage in human sacrifice because they believe it is the will of Artemis. The goddess is conveniently silent on the issue, but the ritual to honour Artemis prescribed in the closing scene, with the requirement to draw blood from a man's throat (1459–60), suggests that the goddess does require an offering of human blood. Henceforth this will be symbolic rather than lethal.

Male and female roles

Greek tragedy was written, produced, financed and performed exclusively by men at Athens, and the number of women who attended the theatrical performances will have been very small.[33] Athenian women had no independent civic rights, and were always subject to a *kyrios*, literally 'a validator', who was a male relative, most commonly a father or a husband. Only male Athenian citizens held the right to take part in political life. Athenian women were not even allowed to appear in court on their own behalf but had to be represented by a man, normally their male *kyrios*.[34] It is remarkable, then, that Greek tragedy gives such prominent roles to female characters, and it has been argued that Greek tragedy's obsession with 'uncontrollable' women stems from the patriarchy's fear of unsupervised female activity.[35] Only one surviving Greek tragedy (Sophocles' *Philoctetes*) has an all-male cast of characters, and the most recognizable of all Greek tragic roles are female ones – Antigone, Medea, Phaedra, Hecuba, Clytemnestra. Each of these tragic characters is complex in their own way. Sophocles' Antigone defies her uncle Creon, the new head of state, and transgresses his edict not to bury her dead brother Polynices who had attacked the city. In doing so, she rejects her fiancé and the opportunity of marriage and performs what she believes to be her ritual duty. Although she dies, the seer Tiresias reveals to a broken Creon at the end of the play that the gods did require the burial of Polynices, implying that Antigone was right to do so. Euripides' Medea, on the other hand, is betrayed by her spineless husband, who leaves her and their two sons in order to marry the local princess for his own self-advancement. Her many sympathizers in the play agree that she has been treated badly by him. The king of Athens offers her sanctuary partly for this reason, but the revenge she hatches is brutal. She murders the local king and his daughter, using her sons as accessories, and then kills the two boys before flying off in the chariot of her grandfather, the Sun god, her revenge apparently effected with divine approval. Phaedra, meanwhile, in Euripides' *Hippolytus* is struck down with lust for her step-son Hippolytus by the goddess Aphrodite. When her secret is revealed, she commits suicide leaving a letter accusing Hippolytus (falsely) of rape. The accusation is believed by her husband Theseus, who calls down Poseidon's curse on his son, thus causing his death. In Euripides' *Hecuba*, the enslaved queen of Troy, Hecuba manages to exact revenge on the Thracian king who had murdered her son by killing his own two sons and blinding him. Aeschylus's Clytemnestra also exacts a terrible revenge for the death of her child Iphigenia, by murdering her husband Agamemnon, though she is later unable to save herself from death at the hands of her son and becomes a ghost urging her Furies to pursue him in the final play of the *Oresteia* trilogy.

All of these female characters find ways to wield power, and their female identities as sisters or wives or mothers is stressed differently in each play. What makes Iphigenia so unique in *Iphigenia among the Taurians* is that she is not a dangerous tragic female in any typical manner. She does not actively seek to threaten or endanger men. Rather, she is forced, against her will, to preside over the deaths of Greek men in the performance of a ritual which is abhorrent to her. The power she holds, moreover, is entirely legitimate and comes from her priestly office. Serving in one of the established female priesthoods would have been the only possible opportunity for an Athenian woman to hold public office. So prestigious was the authority associated therewith that it has even been argued that Athenian priestesses were exempt from requiring a *kyrios* to litigate, and could bring cases to court in their own right.[36] The most celebrated female priesthoods were those of Athena Polias at Athens, Demeter and Persephone at Eleusis, Hera at Argos, and Apollo at Delphi. The first three came with cultic eponymy, meaning that political events were dated according to the names of the priestesses who officiated. The forty-eighth year of Chrysis' service as priestess at Argos, for example, is one of the references used by Thucydides to date the beginning of the Peloponnesian War (Thuc. 2.2.1). The priesthood of Athena Polias was hereditary and was held by members of one of the oldest Athenian aristocratic families, the Eteoboutadai. Its priestesses were married and held the office for life. The priesthood of Demeter and Kore was open to married women with children. It was associated with the Philleidai clan and was known to generate significant income for its priestess. It is not clear whether tenure was for life or whether priestesses came exclusively from this clan, but the office does not seem to have been hereditary. The priesthood of Hera at Argos also seems to have been open to married women, though little concrete information about this office survives. The most prominent of all female priesthoods was that of the Pythia. She was in charge of communicating the oracular responses of Apollo at Delphi, which gave her enormous influence since the oracle was consulted by both individuals and government representatives from all over the Greek world on matters personal and strategic, respectively. The Pythia was chosen from a community of women who were not aristocratic. She was an older woman, and was required to remain celibate after taking office, which was held for life.[37]

The Pythia appears briefly as a character in Aeschylus's *Eumenides* (1–93), whose opening scenes are set in front of the temple of Apollo at Delphi, and in Euripides' *Ion* (1320–68) which takes place in its entirety before the Delphic temple of Apollo. Only in *Iphigenia among the Taurians*, however, do we have a priestess in the main role.[38] Iphigenia holds the temple key (131, cf. 1463), which must have been part of her costume, and was the 'surest signifier of feminine priestly status in [Greek] visual culture' (see cover image).[39] Evidence for female priesthoods of Artemis suggests that they were held by unmarried young women before they transitioned to marriage.[40] The fact that Iphigenia fails to achieve this transition, as we discussed in Chapter 2, is thus underlined by the anomalous nature of her priesthood to Artemis, which must continue in perpetuity at Brauron until her death, after the end of the play. Nevertheless, Iphigenia's identity as a priestess gives her an extraordinary degree of *positive* authority for a Greek tragic heroine. The office allows Iphigenia to wield power in a prominent yet socially acceptable manner. Moreover it explains, in Greek sociological terms, why Thoas and the Taurians follow Iphigenia's instructions unquestioningly. Iphigenia is not associated with masculine qualities the way her powerful mother, Clytemnestra, had been in Aeschylus's negative portrayal. Indeed, Euripides seems to go out of his way to draw an explicit contrast between Aeschylus's Clytemnestra and his own Iphigenia. When Orestes asks Iphigenia, 'Will you, a female, kill me, a male, yourself with a sword?' (621), she answers 'No', explaining that she consecrates the victims for sacrifice with sprinklings of lustral water, but others carry out the killing (622–4). Orestes' question evokes the Aeschylean anomaly of Clytemnestra who is 'a female murderer of the male' (*Ag.* 1231) and who is said to have used a sword (*Ag.* 1351, 1529). The anomaly does not repeat itself in the subsequent generation.[41]

Orestes depends on Iphigenia to fulfil his quest and escape. Asking for her assistance to steal the statue, Orestes pleads desperately, 'O loved one, o dearest sister, save our ancestral house and save me!' (983–4). Iphigenia proves herself intellectually superior to Orestes during the plotting scene. Dismissing Orestes' proposal of killing the king, she conceives instead a highly convincing ruse to ensure their escape under the king's nose and with his unwitting complicity. The traits exhibited by the siblings in this scene are gendered in broad strokes. Men tend towards violent action, where women are clever schemers, an intellectual extension of their skill at weaving.[42] So Orestes connects Iphigenia's cleverness with her gender (1031), while the Taurian Messenger associates it with female deception (1298). However, these apparently gendered associations are flexible. Odysseus is a schemer *par excellence* whose masculinity is not in question. Within the play, Iphigenia's deception mirrors that of Odysseus at Aulis as Laura McClure has noticed.[43] Conversely, women in Greek literature can become wildly aggressive in certain circumstances without any association with masculine behaviour. Maenads, for example, who were female followers of Dionysus, were believed to have the ability to rip apart their hunted prey, as is dramatized to devastating effect in Euripides' *Bacchae* where Agave dismembers her own son in the mistaken belief that he is a mountain lion.

It is clear in *Iphigenia among the Taurians* that Orestes is wholly dependent on Iphigenia for his survival and escape, and that Iphigenia is very much in control of events. The play, however, is not evidence of some kind of proto-feminism. Rather, Iphigenia is made to express the sort of misogynist sentiments that commonly feature in Greek literature. She is determined to help Orestes escape, even if she dies in the attempt, because 'the fact is, a man who dies is longed for by the house, but a woman is of no consequence' (1004–5). The sentiment echoes the imagery of Iphigenia's dream where male children are identified as the 'pillars' of the house (57–8). Such expressions of the higher social value of male offspring are nevertheless thought-provoking within the context of the play's emphasis on the theme of birth, which naturally stresses the value of motherhood for society and for culture. That focus also has the effect of redressing another anomaly proposed in Aeschylus's *Oresteia*, where Apollo had put forward a completely bogus biological argument suggesting that the father alone was the true 'parent', and the mother simply a vessel, in order to mitigate Orestes' crime of matricide (*Eum.* 657–73). The proposition is tacitly validated by Athena, who was born fully grown from Zeus's head, when she announces that she is siding with the male in all respects (*Eum.* 734–41). In *Iphigenia among the Taurians*, by contrast, childbirth and motherhood are insistently connected, both in the mortal world and in the divine realm, and work to undermine the resolution of Aeschylus's *Oresteia*.[44]

At the end of the drama's opening song, Iphigenia, whose name in Greek means 'strong in birth', had given extended consideration to the night of her own birth. She had suggested that she was ill-fated from that moment (203–13), had lamented her own childlessness (220), and had concluded with fond memories of Orestes as a breast-feeding infant in his mother's arms (231–5). This tender image stresses the atrocity of Orestes' crime of matricide, of which Iphigenia is as yet unaware. It is notable, however, that when Iphigenia questions Orestes and Pylades about their identity, she first asks them if they have the same mother (497), only subsequently asking what name their father gave them (499). In Athens, fathers would name (and so legitimize) their children in a ceremony conducted ten days after their birth,[45] but, in the formulation of Iphigenia's questions, motherhood (and thus childbirth) is given priority over paternal acknowledgement. Orestes is at first evasive about his identity, but he later reveals to

Iphigenia's distress that Clytemnestra was killed by the son she bore (556). After the recognition scene, Iphigenia comes to understand that Orestes is pursued by his mother's Furies because of the matricide (924–33). The issues of birth and of the maternal bond are, in a general sense, always going to be relevant to the story of Orestes. In Aeschylus's *Libation Bearers* (896–8), Clytemnestra had dramatically exposed her breast to emphasize that bond as a desperate, and ultimately unsuccessful, attempt to save her own life. In *Iphigenia among the Taurians*, however, the importance of the goddess Artemis, one of whose spheres of patronage is childbirth, provides a new dimension to the theme. The Chorus pine for Artemis the 'birth-bringer' (1097), while Iphigenia questions the notion that Leto could have given birth to a goddess (Artemis) who rejects the blood pollution of childbirth but delights in human sacrifices (380–6). As Artemis's servant, Iphigenia is concerned that pregnant women should avoid the pollution of matricide (1228).

The birth of Leto's other child, Artemis's twin brother Apollo, is the subject of the Chorus's final song (1234–83). He was born on the island of Delos (1235) and, as Edith Hall reminds us, this island had been purified by the Athenians in 426 BCE.[46] They had dug up and removed the remains of all who were buried there and decreed that no births or deaths should take place on the island in the future (Thuc. 3.104). The event, which must have been familiar to the audience of *Iphigenia among the Taurians*, converges with significant issues of the play – death, pollution and purification, and birth. The choral song describes how Apollo, as an infant, was brought by his mother to Delphi and came into possession of the oracle thereby ousting its female occupant, the goddess Themis ('Righteousness'). When Themis' mother Gaia ('Earth') comes to her aid, by 'giving birth' (1262) to prophetic dreams for mortals, and so making Apollo's prophecies redundant, Apollo seeks the assistance of his father Zeus and wins out. Christiane Sourvinou-Inwood observed that the mother–

daughter relationship in this song is implicitly compared with the father–son relationship, and represented as inferior.[47] It is also the case that the Olympian gods subdue the older chthonic female divinities, as in the *Oresteia*. The significance of childbearing as a theme, however, continues into the play's conclusion since Iphigenia is to be subsumed into the cult of Artemis at Brauron after her death, where she will receive dedications of clothes belonging to women who died in childbirth (1462–7). The rituals prescribed by Athena thus reflect the gendered value placed on men and women in Greek society. Men were expected to risk their lives for the city by going to war if necessary. The equivalent sacrifice made by women was giving birth to new citizens in an age when childbirth was hazardous and could be fatal. Iphigenia is to be associated with these dangers. From presiding over the deaths of men, her authority is transferred to the realm of deceased women. As Barbara Goff has noted, this conclusion means that Iphigenia no longer represents a threat to men and the play thus conforms to the familiar pattern in Greek tragedy where the danger posed by females is ultimately neutralized.[48] Meanwhile, Orestes is to found a ritual that includes holding a sword at a man's throat and drawing blood (1459–60). On one level, this is a symbolic representation of the kind of death a Greek male might suffer in combat.

The resolution of the play validates both male and female contributions to civic life, though we are reminded of the physical superiority of men in the report of the attempted escape. In a surprising detail, our plucky heroine Iphigenia has not been able to get onto the ship because she is afraid of getting her foot wet. So Orestes lifts her onto his shoulder, goes into the sea and climbs up the ladder, placing his sister with the statue safely onto the ship (1380–3). For a modern audience, quite used to dominant, intelligent and physically able heroines, this may seem out of character for Iphigenia. After all the bravery and intelligence she has demonstrated, she is now apparently afraid of stepping into the sea. This would be unfathomable in a twenty-first century action and adventure plot. Is it possible that Iphigenia cannot swim? This is not specified, but if we assume that this is the case then the moment may also engage with ethnic stereotypes. As Edith Hall has discussed, Greek achievements in swimming and diving were 'symbolic of Greek victory over the barbarians', particularly after the defeat of the Persians at sea during the Persian Wars.[49] Athenians reportedly taught their children to swim and young women were not necessarily excluded from this education. A diver Skyllis and his daughter Hydne, whom he had trained, were honoured at Delphi with a dedication for their service in the Greek cause against the Persians when they caused havoc for the Persian fleet by dragging up their anchor lines and moorings during a storm.[50] Plato's Athenian references a saying which groups ignorance of letters and swimming together as markers of the most uneducated person (*Laws* 3.689d3). The connection is interesting when we consider that Iphigenia did not write her own letter and did not seem to read it, but rather paraphrased its contents (see Chapter 1). Perhaps, for all her intellectual skill and ritual authority, Iphigenia has remained ignorant of letters and unable to swim. If this is how we are to interpret Iphigenia's fear of stepping into the sea, then Euripides is once again playing with ethnic stereotypes since Greek literature normally associates an inability to swim with barbarians.[51]

In the context of *Iphigenia among the Taurians*' relationship with the *Oresteia*, it makes sense that male valour be restored at the end of the play. Nevertheless, even if the value of masculine strength is brought to the fore in the Messenger's report of Orestes hoisting Iphigenia onto the ship along with the precious statue of Artemis, the theme of gender relations is resolved with a significant degree of equilibrium, which reflects the parallel sufferings of the siblings.[52] In order to move forward with the escape, Iphigenia depends on Orestes' physical strength, and indeed on his ship, just as much as he has depended on her plan. Moreover, the escape of the siblings will only be assured through divine intervention, which ultimately mitigates human efforts, either male or female.

Conclusion

In *Iphigenia among the Taurians*, Euripides interrogates ethnically determined cultural practices and investigates socially prescribed gender roles. The play is unusual in granting such positive and culturally acceptable authority to a female protagonist. Although the play ultimately conforms to the Greek tragic pattern of reasserting patriarchal order, there is an important and arguably unparalleled emphasis on the positive value of women's contributions to civic society, both through ritual practices and through childbirth. Where ethnicity is concerned, the issue is not entirely straightforward. The Taurians direct their aggression outside their own community, while the Greeks engage in internecine violence.[53] This suggests that the Greeks are ironically more barbaric than the 'barbarians', but binary oppositions do not capture the full picture and we should not presume that the Taurians were to be admired more than the Greek characters by Euripides' audience. The Athens of Greek tragedy often accepts into its community outcasts from other Greek cities in a magnanimous fashion. The legendary king of Athens, Theseus, welcomes Heracles who has murdered his family (at the end of Euripides' *Heracles*), and Oedipus the parricide who had married his mother (at the end of Sophocles' *Oedipus at Colonus*). Medea manipulates Theseus' father Aegeus into granting her sanctuary (in Euripides' *Medea*). Orestes, of course, is also such a figure. He recounts his reception at Athens in *Iphigenia among the Taurians* (939–78), and the cult which he must found at Halai will secure a lasting connection between Orestes and Athens. Iphigenia will remain in Athenian environs for life. So although Taurian hostility to strangers can be explained as a Taurian custom (*nomos*), it will have remained a negative characteristic for an Athenian audience. Similarly, the unquestioning piety of the Taurians may have had desultory connotations in the context of Euripides' proclivity for philosophically engaged characters who tend to challenge conceptions of the gods in their traditional forms. As we shall see in the next chapter, Iphigenia is one such character, and the issue of divine design is a central conundrum of the play.

4

Ritual and the Gods

Ritual actions, such as making offerings to the gods or conducting funerary rites, and ritual speech, such as prayers, curses and oaths, are central to the fabric of Greek tragedy.[1] As we noted briefly in Chapter 1, Greek tragedy itself was performed at a religious festival in honour of Dionysus, patron god of drama. This festival, called the City Dionysia, was held annually in the spring over the course of several days. Immediately preceding the festival, a procession took place commemorating the first arrival of the god Dionysus to Athens. The cult statue was taken from the temple on the southern slope of the Acropolis to a grove outside the city where hymns were sung and sacrifices made in honour of the god. Once these proceedings had concluded, the statue was returned to the theatre with a torch-lit parade. A second procession opened the official festival and included representatives from different categories of Athenian life carrying provisions for the sacrifice and feast. It was led by a virgin of aristocratic background holding a golden basket with sacrificial offerings. Male citizens carried wine and bread. Metics (resident aliens) also carried provisions and their daughters carried water jugs. Ephebes (young men of military age) led a bull, which was the main sacrificial animal. Groups of men sang hymns and carried large phalluses, indicative of Dionysus' fertility. Competitions in a specific type of choral song and dance, called the dithyramb, were held, with each of the ten tribes of Athens supplying choruses of fifty men and fifty boys.[2] The competitive dramatic performances followed over the course of several days. These were preceded by the ritual purification of the theatre and a libation of wine offered by the ten generals of

Athens. Several ceremonial actions of civic importance also took place, including the naming of distinguished citizens and benefactors, the display of tribute sent to Athens by allied states, and the honouring of war orphans.[3]

The ritual activities of the City Dionysia festival include elements that were typical of Greek religious practices: a formal procession, here escorting the cult statue of a god; singing hymns; sacrificing animals; a purification ceremony; and the pouring of libations.[4] With the substitution of humans for animals, all of these rituals either take place or are in evidence in *Iphigenia among the Taurians*. That is not to say that the drama is mimetic of events at City Dionysia festival.[5] Rather, the types of ritual activity which occur in the play, again with the exception of human sacrifice, would have been very familiar to an Athenian audience. This drama is, moreover, particularly laden with ritual referents. As Barbara Goff has observed, the materiality of ritual is stressed through the temple setting, the altar, the libation poured by Iphigenia, and the statue of Artemis, but also through Iphigenia's lament that she is unable to weave images of Athena defeating the Titans (222–4).[6] This allusion is a reference to the Athenian practice of offering a robe to Athena, woven by young women, at the Panathenaic festival.[7] We shall see, in our discussion of human sacrifice, and of the relationship between Artemis and Iphigenia, how important normative Greek religious practices are for comprehending the drama's abnormal scenario. The play's conclusion focuses audience attention on acceptable rituals condoned by Athena at Halai and Brauron. In fact, *Iphigenia among the Taurians* is also the surviving Greek tragedy that contains the greatest number of ritual aetiologies, or mythological explanations for the cause (*aition*) of a specific ritual practice. In addition to the aetiologies for the worship of Artemis at Halai and Brauron, we are presented with a foundation myth for the *Choes* festival honouring Dionysus. Scholars disagree over the extent to which these cult aetiologies reflected actual rituals,[8] but the aetiologies certainly refer to real locations and recognizable types of ritual as will be discussed in more detail below.

There is a further lack of scholarly consensus regarding the significance of Dionysiac worship for experiencing tragedy.[9] Attending the dramatic performances was not in itself an act of worship. Nevertheless, it remains incontestable that all Greek tragedy is saturated with references to religious language and ritual. The gods themselves are often cast as characters performing roles, either instigating or resolving the action, particularly in the dramas of Euripides. The subject of Euripides' representation of the gods has been much discussed by scholars. In recent decades, some have focused on the cultural contexts of Euripides' representation of religion.[10] Others have stressed the reciprocal relationships between the gods and humans in Euripides.[11] Human characters in Euripidean drama frequently question divine actions and challenge traditional religious thought, which led influential nineteenth-century figures, such as Nietzsche and the Schlegel brothers, to promote a view that Euripides was an atheist or a rationalist, often drawing selectively from Euripides' work and from parodic representations of Euripides in the comedies of Aristophanes to support their positions.[12] Several scholars have challenged such conceptions, by arguing that the role of the gods has serious implications for the human characters in Euripides' plays, and that the divine in Euripides is essentially bleak and traditional.[13] Euripidean theology proves to be so elusive because, while his plays do contain rationalizing and often highly convincing arguments regarding the nature of the gods, these are invariably shown to be mistaken at the drama's conclusion. In *Hippolytus*, for example, the Servant prays to Aphrodite to overlook Hippolytus' folly, suggesting that gods should be wiser than mortals (120), but we know from Aphrodite's appearance in the prologue that she has already planned her revenge on Hippolytus and this is confirmed by Artemis in the final scene (*Hipp.* 21–3, 1400). A similar pattern occurs in *Iphigenia among the Taurians* where

Iphigenia refuses to believe that Artemis truly desires human sacrifices, but a ritual involving the shedding of human blood in honour of Artemis (albeit symbolic rather than fatal) is prescribed by Athena in the play's conclusion. If we focus on the divine authority that frequently closes a Euripidean play, we are forced to conclude, pessimistically, that the will of the gods is arbitrary, inscrutable and can be cruel. The human intellect, which attempts to make sense of the divine, then becomes at best irrelevant and at worst a failure. The approach taken here, however, will be to examine how rational human thought and divine action function together within the drama as a whole. It will be argued that the arbitrary actions of the gods, forced upon the plot, do not provide satisfactory conclusions to the theological questions raised and must therefore be designed to prompt further audience reflection on these issues.

Human sacrifice, Artemis and Iphigenia

Exploration of the concept of human sacrifice has been identified as a particularly Euripidean theme.[14] As we noted in Chapter 2, however, other tragedies represent the voluntary sacrifice of the young for the perceived good of the community. *Iphigenia among the Taurians* is unique in extant Euripides in representing *unwilling* sacrificial victims, both in the reports of Iphigenia's sacrifice and in the sacrifices of stray Greeks. The fact that Artemis apparently requires Iphigenia's sacrifice does not negate its deleterious impact. The ancient Greeks would have been familiar with the ritual sacrificial slaughter of animals, whose throats were slit in a ceremonial fashion. The primary function of animal sacrifice was to provide food for the community, and the trappings of ceremony associated therewith functioned to free those conducting the sacrifice from guilt. Metaphors taken from animal sacrifice are often manipulated in disturbing ways in Greek tragedy, with the ultimate distortion being human sacrifice.[15] Jan Bremmer has recently traced the use of ritual vocabulary in our play. Human sacrifice in *Iphigenia among the Taurians* proceeds analogously to Greek animal sacrifice, but with some significant anomalies. The victim is prepared with sprinklings of lustral water (53–4, 58, 243–5, 334, 662), and 'consecrations' (244), which refer to the sprinkling of barley groats on the victim and the cutting of hair with the sacrificial knife. So far this is identical to preparations for animal sacrifice. As Bremmer notes, however, the victim's throat will be cut with a sword, rather than with the usual sacrificial knife. This connects the human sacrifices taking place among the Taurians with the sacrifice of Iphigenia at Aulis and stresses a military context. Most significantly, the victim is not consumed but will be burned as a holocaust.[16]

Although there are a small number of references to human sacrifice in historical sources, there is no archaeological evidence to confirm that the Greeks ever practised human sacrifice. In his *Life of Themistocles* (13.2–5), Plutarch, writing in the first to second centuries CE, claimed that the Athenian general Themistocles sacrificed three captive young men before the Battle of Salamis in 480 BCE. However, there are serious reasons for doubting the authenticity of the story and the reliability of Plutarch's source.[17] Nevertheless, it has been argued that the classical Greeks believed that human sacrifices had occurred in their distant past and that the idea of human sacrifice as a concept was important throughout antiquity.[18] There is no archaeological evidence either for a practice of human sacrifice in the Tauric Chersonese.[19] In Euripides, we are asked to consider whether or not the goddess Artemis really requires human sacrifice. Or do humans excuse their own wickedness by attributing it to the gods? (398–90). It is the question we are left with at the end of the play, and one to which we will return.

The case of Iphigenia in the Taurian tragedy is unique for another reason. The Greeks believe she is dead, although her life has actually been saved by Artemis. Iphigenia has paradoxically experienced the horror of being prepared for sacrifice, while escaping the fatal blow through the substitution of a deer (28). In the representation of Iphigenia's miraculous survival, moreover, a conflation between Artemis and Iphigenia is implied. Iphigenia was commonly conflated with Artemis in Greek thought and in Athenian cult.[20] Herodotus' Taurians offer human sacrifices to the Virgin goddess (Parthenos), who is identified as Iphigenia, rather than Artemis (Hdt. 4.103.9–10). In Euripides, both are addressed as *potnia* 'lady' (463, 533, 1082, 1123), called 'maiden' (402, 1114), and are associated with cleverness (380, 1031). The goddess and her servant arrive among the Taurians in parallel fashion. The statue of Artemis is said to have fallen from the sky into the temple (87–8), while Iphigenia has been 'stolen' and transported through the bright air and established in the temple (28–34). Iphigenia and Artemis's stolen statue will make the same return journey to Greece on board the ship of Orestes.[21] The statue is identified by three different Greek terms: *xoanon bretas* and *agalma*. A *xoanon* was a polished or carved statuette, plain but ancient and particularly sacred, imbued with divine presence, while an *agalma*, literally 'an adornment', was typically a more contemporary sculptural artwork. A *bretas*, like the *xoanon*, suggests an archaic image.[22] Although the terms seem to be used interchangeably in the play, with *xoanon* used only once (1359), it is clear that the statue is ancient. The repeated reference to the *agalma* of Artemis, then, may also evoke the famous description of Iphigenia, about to be sacrificed in Aeschylus's *Agamemnon* (208) where, as Laura McClure reminds us, she is called *domōn agalma* 'the adornment of the house'.[23] We may add that Iphigenia goes into the *domōn* 'house' of Artemis at the beginning of the play (65). The temple is a 'house' because the deity is believed to dwell in the sanctuary through the cult statue, and the language simultaneously associates female ritual authority with domestic space.[24] Thus, both Iphigenia and the statue of Artemis can be conceptualized as *domōn agalma* 'the adornment of the house', further confirming a conflation between them.

The fact that the statue of Artemis is imagined as being alive is exploited by Iphigenia in her deception of Thoas. She tells him that the statue turned backwards in its seat of its own accord and closed its eyes (1165–7), rejecting the polluted victims. The purification ritual in the sea recalls the washing of the cult statue of Athena Polias at the Plynteria festival, as we noted in Chapter 1. Ultimately, Iphigenia will be worshipped along with Artemis at Brauron, forever linked to her patron, but it is Athena who resolves the action of the play, and we should not forget that the actor who played Iphigenia will also have played Athena. This may have consolidated a sense of conflation between the mortal Iphigenia and a female divinity, and Barbara Goff has observed that Athena announces her instructions as *epistolai* (1446), which means both 'commands' and 'written letters'. These *epistolai* reach the ears of the absent adresses Orestes and Pylades by miraculous means, and suggest a parallel to Iphigenia's own miraculous letter delivery.[25]

Halai and Brauron

Worship of Artemis at Halai and Brauron is firmly attested. Her sanctuary at Brauron was situated on the eastern coast of Attica near the Aegean Sea, while the deme of Halai lay further up the coast, six kilometres north of Brauron. Details given in *Iphigenia among the Taurians* regarding cult practices to be established there are likely to have been invention, albeit variants of recognizable types of pre-existing rituals. The difficulty with relating Euripidean aetiologies to actual cult practice, however, comes down to a chicken and egg scenario. All sources which might corroborate Euripidean aetiologies postdate *Iphigenia among the Taurians* and may well have been influenced by the drama. Moreover, the evidence we do have for cult worship at Halai and Brauron in the fifth century BCE seems to bear little connection to the rituals described in Euripides. What we can say for certain is that Euripidean aetiology has had an enormous impact on later assessments of worship at these sites.

There is frustratingly little evidence surviving for activities at Halai, more properly called Halai Araphenides (located near modern-day Loutsa). A temple of Artemis existed at the site in the fifth century BCE, and there is evidence of religious activity here dating back to the Bronze Age.[26] It is only in the later fifth century BCE, however, that the site becomes associated with Artemis Tauropolos. The epithet Tauropolos was associated particularly with the worship of Artemis in Asia Minor.[27] In Sophocles' *Ajax* (172), dated to the 440s BCE, the Chorus wonder if it was Artemis Tauropolos who caused Ajax's madness. This is noteworthy because Ajax's actions are similar to those of the mad Orestes in Euripides' later *Iphigenia among the Taurians*. Ajax attacks and slaughters a herd of cattle in the mistaken belief that they are his mortal enemies, after Athena drives him mad. As we have seen, Orestes similarly attacks and slaughters a herd of cattle believing that they are the Furies causing his madness. Although Artemis is not actually involved in either event, it is clear that she can be associated with such scenarios, not least through her role as both protector and destroyer of animals. The epithet Tauropolos means 'bull-herder' and relates also to Artemis's role as the patron of young males in their prime.[28] Euripides was fond of word play and the etymology he concocts here is contrived.[29] It is suggested that Artemis is named Tauropolos for the land of the Taurians and for Orestes' 'roaming', since 'to roam' is a possible meaning of the verb *poleō* from which *-polos* derives. It is possible that Euripides generated this connection with the Black Sea Taurians in acknowledgement of increasing Athenian dependence on grain trade with the Black Sea at the end of the fifth century BCE, implicitly identifying the Greek

Artemis with the Taurian Parthenos (Virgin Goddess), also a patron of animals and hunting.[30] In any case, the mock death ritual prescribed by Athena in honour of Artemis Tauropolos, a substitution for Orestes' actual death to be undergone by young men in the future (1458–61), may suggest a type of male initiation ritual into the adult community.[31] The bloodshed would mark the symbolic transition of a young man into a warrior. Martin Cropp suggests that this 'probably provided an origin (*aition*) for a real ritual', but we cannot be certain.[32] This issue is further complicated by the other significant information we have about the Tauropolia festival, which seems to bear no relation to what is described in Euripides.

In the comedy *The Litigants* by Menander (c. 300 BCE), the Tauropolia festival is represented as an all-night revel, attended by young women as well as young men, with music, dancing and drinking. The plot turns on the rape of a young woman by a drunken young man during the festival. It seems impossible to reconcile these two accounts of the worship of Artemis Tauropolos, even if, in outline, both festivals, rape aside, reflect common types of worship in classical Greece. A report of interest in this context survives in the work of the second-century CE travel writer Pausanias (3.16.7–11). He claims that the sacred statue of Artemis Tauropolos was actually located in the sanctuary of Artemis Orthia in Sparta. There, young men were reportedly whipped with blood drawn, while they tried to steal cheese from Artemis's altar. The motifs of symbolic blood-letting and theft provide strong connections between this ritual and the ritual prescribed by Athena in Euripides' play, bearing in mind Orestes' original theft of the statue.[33] It must be conceded that the two sources are separated by several centuries, but Jeremy McInerney suggests that the ritual mentioned in Pausanias may be alluded to in Xenophon's fourth-century BCE *Spartan Constitution* (2.8–9), where it is reported that the Spartans scourge thieves who are caught stealing cheese.[34] As a final piece to this puzzle, there is evidence to suggest that the *pyrrhichē*, a stylized war dance competitively performed by young men, formed part of the Tauropolia festival, at least in the later fourth century BCE.[35] This evidence once again postdates Euripides, but it would seem to forge a connection between the aspect of dancing mentioned in Menander and the transition of young males into men of warrior status suggested by the Euripidean aetiology.

About Brauron, we have more consistent information, though again there is little ostensible correlation between what is known of cultic activity at Brauron and what is prescribed in Euripides. Artemis was worshipped there, and there was also a sanctuary to Brauronian Artemis on the southwestern side of the Athenian Acropolis, 'an urban twin of the goddess's rural sanctuary at Brauron'.[36] At Brauron itself, the *arkteia* 'festival of the bears' was held every four years, where girls who had not yet reached menarche 'became bears' and served in the temple of Artemis for a period of time. The festival was a rite of passage, marking the transition of girls from childhood to puberty in anticipation of their readiness for marriage.[37] The ritual was probably related to a substitution myth like the one associated with the worship of Artemis at Mounichia where an *arkteia* took place every year. Artemis had demanded the sacrifice of a girl as compensation for the death of a sacred bear. A man called Embaros vowed to sacrifice his daughter to Artemis to rid his city of affliction, but he hid his daughter in the temple and dressed a goat in her clothes, offering the she-goat as the sacrificial victim. The offering was accepted and human sacrifice was avoided.[38] A similarity of motif suggests itself with the myth of Iphigenia, which is also one of substitution where Artemis had replaced her with a deer on the sacrificial altar, and Angeliki Tzanetou has argued that the plot of *Iphigenia among the Taurians* should be read against the rituals of the *arkteia*.[39] Several scholars have posited that Iphigenia received cult at Brauron in one of the buildings of the sanctuary complex. However, as Gunnel Ekroth has shown in his careful and detailed analysis of both archaeological and literary evidence, these arguments are essentially circular. Iphigenia's presence at Brauron is inferred from Euripides' text but archaeological finds do not actually support this conclusion.[40] We know from inscriptions preserved at Brauron that women commonly dedicated clothes to Artemis there, and might do so as an offering in gratitude for a successful birth.[41] Iphigenia, on the other hand, is due to receive dedications of clothes belonging to women who *died* in childbirth, according to Euripides, and there are 'no known parallels to this kind of ritual practice anywhere else in the Greek world'.[42] Maria Mirto observes that the experience of these women combines the two kinds of pollution, from death and from childbirth, that are said to be rejected by Artemis in the play (381–3), and the commemorative dedications will be received, not by Artemis herself, but by Iphigenia.[43] The horror of Orestes' matricide, Froma Zeitlin notes, is 'naturalized, as it were' by the tragic but common death of women in childbirth.[44]

The rituals prescribed for Halai and Brauron follow the pattern of male and female initiation rites, respectively, as Hugh Lloyd-Jones argued.[45] We must nevertheless conclude, however, that Euripides has manipulated established Greek ritual practices and introduced his own invented details in order to emphasize certain significant aspects of his drama. The rituals that are to take place at Halai and Brauron are uncanny, and Ekroth notices that, like the dedications of offerings from deceased women at Brauron, the drawing of human blood with a sword at Halai is similarly 'an action which has no parallel in other Greek cults'.[46] It becomes clear, thematically, what is at stake. Iphigenia, whose name means 'strong in birth', and who has longed to complete her transition to marriage and motherhood, is fated to remain unable to complete that transition and will continue to live in isolation. Having escaped from overseeing the death of men, she will be forever associated with the death of women who have also failed to complete the transition to motherhood. In the case of Orestes, the ritual at Halai confirms that the gods do require an offering of human blood, contrary to normal Greek religious practice. Moreover, the cult must be established through an act of theft which, under normal circumstances, would have been considered a sacrilegious crime carrying serious penalties, including death, if convicted.[47] Iphigenia is aware of this since she fears Artemis may disapprove of the theft and asks Artemis to pardon it (995–8, 1012–14, 1400). These anomalous elements in Euripidean cultic aetiologies serve to underline the dark undercurrent in the drama's conclusion, which suggests that the nature of the gods and of divine design is implacable and inscrutable. In the case of Iphigenia, the prescribed outcome shows that the gods care little for human desires, and while Orestes is to be finally purified and will return to Argos as he had hoped, the ritual at Halai stresses the failure of the positive incorporation of the Furies into Athenian cult, which had been expounded in Aeschylus's *Oresteia*. Euripides makes this explicit in his aetiology of the *Choes* festival to which we now turn.

Choes

The *Choes* ('Beakers') festival, took place on the second day of the *Anthesteria*, an annual wine festival held in honour of Dionysus. It was the most important day in the three-day festival, which involved the consumption of the new year's wine. It was preceded by the *Pithoigia* 'Opening of the wine casks', and followed by the day of the *Chytroi* 'Pots'.[48] Orestes in *Iphigenia among the Taurians* describes the foundation of the *Choes* festival as follows (939–78). After killing his mother he is sent by Apollo to stand trial for his crime at Athens. When he arrives in Athens, none of his *xenoi* 'guest-friends' was at first willing to receive him 'a man detested by the gods' (948). Those who felt obliged to honour their bond of friendship provided him with a separate table, where he was given food and drink but left alone and shunned. Each of the other diners drank equal measures of wine from their own beakers (953–4). This detail is significant because Greeks normally shared communal drinking cups at feasts.[49] The use of individual cups is here associated by Euripides with Orestes' pollution and the fear of contagion. Orestes suffers in silence during this experience, and then says he has heard that the Athenians have made a ritual from his misfortunes in a festival with individual beakers. In the latter part of the speech, Orestes recounts how he stood trial at Athens and was acquitted thanks to Athena's support. The Furies accepted this judgement and settled in Athens in a new sanctuary established for them, but some of them were unpersuaded by the legal process and continued to hound Orestes. Going in desperation back to Apollo's temple, Orestes threatens to starve himself in the sanctuary and die there if Apollo does not save him. It was at this point that he received the oracle to go to the land of the Taurians and return to Greece with the statue of Artemis.

Orestes' account thus alludes directly to the conclusion of Aeschylus's *Oresteia*, where Orestes had stood trial and was acquitted thanks to Athena persuading the Furies to take up residence in Athens where they will receive honours. Aeschylus makes Orestes' trial the first trial for homicide to take place on the Areopagus, thus creating a foundation myth for the homicide court at Athens.[50] Euripides, however, refers to a variant (945–6) according to which the court was established by Zeus to try Ares who had pollution on his hands. Moreover, he prefaces the reference to Aeschylus with his own aetiology for the *Choes* festival, and follows it with a direct rejection of Aeschylean theology. The Furies are not unanimously convinced to abandon their prey. Rather a number of Furies remain undomesticated and continue to pursue the killer on behalf of the victim. Euripides thus stresses the inescapability of pollution resulting from matricide.

In attempting to relate what Euripides describes with actual Athenian practices, and in trying to identify what Euripides may have invented, we are faced with the usual problems of evidence for Greek religion. We can nevertheless make some important observations. The only reference to the *Choes* which predates Euripides comes in Aristophanes' comedy *Acharnians* (1000–1232), produced in 425 BCE. It involves a drinking competition and a major feast, but shares with Euripides the significant detail that all participants have their own individual drinking cups. *Acharnians* also mentions a drunken 'mad Orestes' (1167), and while it is not possible to identify this Orestes as the son of Agamemnon from Greek mythology, the figure is certainly intriguing. It may even be that Euripides was inspired by this other Orestes to make the connection with Orestes the matricide. The day of the *Choes* was also associated more generally with the uncanny, with pollution, and with the spirits of the dead.[51] Participants at the *Choes* drinking festival included children (as well as women and slaves) in addition to adult men. Numerous miniature *choes* ('beakers') have survived depicting chubby toddlers and children. A small number of these show young girls, but boys were more prominently involved. The size of the beakers grew with the child and it seems likely that the *Choes* festival marked stages in the journey from childhood towards adulthood, especially for males.[52] If this is the case, then Euripides associates Orestes, who is remembered as an infant by Iphigenia (233–5), with two significant rituals of transition from childhood (the *Choes*) to adulthood (at Halai). At the same time, connecting Orestes with these rituals emphasizes their uncanny aspects.

Divine design and rational intellect

Euripidean theology appears to have two faces. Humans are ultimately revealed as being at the mercy of mysterious and often hostile divine plans. However, Euripidean characters frequently propose radical rationalizing accounts of divine behaviour or religious ritual. In *Iphigenia among the Taurians*, Iphigenia finds fault with Artemis's 'logic' (*sophismata*, 380). The goddess judges those who have had contact with bloodshed, childbirth or death to be polluted and bars them from her altars. At the same time she 'enjoys' human sacrifices (381–4). Iphigenia then declares that Leto could hardly have given birth to such 'mindlessness' (*amathia*, 385–6). The locals, she claims, are themselves murderous and transfer the blame to the goddess (389–90). Within this sequence, Iphigenia inserts an aside concerning her own ancestry. She does not believe in Tantalus's feast for the gods, that the gods 'enjoyed' feeding on his son (386–8). Iphigenia concludes the speech by stating that she does not believe any of the gods to be bad (391).

How are we to interpret these declarations within the framework of the play? Scholars disagree. Some see the general conception of benevolent divinity validated by the outcome of the play and the abolition of human sacrifice.[53] Others, however, have emphasized the continuing violence and bloodshed represented by the new cult of Artemis at Halai.[54] We must also consider the extent to which Artemis had demanded Iphigenia's own sacrifice, and the play is elusive on this point. Stuck at Aulis because of adverse weather, Agamemnon is told by the army's priest Calchas that he will never launch his ships for Troy until Artemis receives his daughter Iphigenia as a sacrifice (15–20). Agamemnon had vowed to offer Artemis the finest thing the year would bear, and Calchas concludes that Iphigenia is that 'finest thing'. It is implied that Agamemnon has a choice, that he might have disbanded the army to save his daughter, a concept that Euripides would develop in his later *Iphigenia at Aulis*. Certainly, Iphigenia stresses the human agency involved in her sacrifice, and it can be argued that since Artemis saved Iphigenia, she did not require or desire a blood sacrifice. At the same time, Iphigenia also claims in this opening speech that Artemis *enjoys* the local rites of human sacrifice (35–6).

The language of 'enjoyment' is significant because it connects Iphigenia's opening remarks to her later rationalization, and to her dismissal of the myth of Tantalus. The insertion of this aside within the primary reflection on the rites of Artemis among the Taurians is a clever piece of sophistry. If it is not possible to determine conclusively whether or not Artemis really does enjoy offerings of human sacrifice, we can be fairly sure that the gods did not 'enjoy' the feast offered by Tantalus. Iphigenia's ancestor had violated his privilege of dining with the gods by dismembering his son Pelops and serving the flesh to his unsuspecting guests. On discovering the abomination, the gods reconstituted Pelops and gave him an ivory shoulder to replace the bite taken by Demeter who had been distracted with mourning the loss of her daughter Persephone. Tantalus was condemned to perpetual punishment in the Underworld. The poet Pindar had also rejected this notion of a cannibalistic feast in *Olympian* 1 (36–63), written to celebrate a horse-racing victory in the Olympic games of 476 BCE, and he has a clear motivation for doing so. Pindar connects his honorand with Pelops who had earned the patronage of Poseidon, god of horsemanship, whose victory in chariot racing had won him his bride, and whose tomb was located near the altar of Zeus at Olympia. In Pindar's version, the atrocious feast never happened at all. Iphigenia, however, seems to accept that the feast took place though she rejects the possibility that the gods enjoyed it.[55] This correlates with the broader argument she puts forward, namely that humans are the ones who commit atrocities. In the case of the Tantalus myth, we may well agree. As regards Artemis, however, the issue remains more difficult to determine. Moreover, the concluding suggestion that gods do not behave badly goes against the entire poetic tradition. In Euripides' *Heracles* (1341–6), the title character expresses similar sentiments rejecting negative stories about the gods, but his own miseries have been brought about because of Hera's jealousy and the plot itself undermines Heracles' positive outlook.

It is not easy to reconcile the two aspects of Euripidean theology, but perhaps that is precisely the point. Thalia Papadopoulou has noticed that the reason it is so difficult to identify the nature and will of Artemis in *Iphigenia among the Taurians* is her own absence and silence on the issue of the human sacrifices held in her honour. In a very different context, the worship of Artemis is central to Euripides' *Hippolytus* where the title character is her devoted servant. In that tragedy, however, Artemis herself appears *ex machina* and has the final word on theological and religious issues. The conclusion of *Iphigenia among the Taurians* is more open-ended in this regard since we are only given Athena's perspective. As Papadopoulou correctly insists, however, this dramatic technique gives the audience a significantly active role in constructing meaning.[56] In fact, *Iphigenia among the Taurians* consistently invites audience interpretation in a number of different ways. Caroline Trieschnigg has shown how Iphigenia's dream engages the audience in a process of interpretation and reinterpretation as expectations for its fulfilment must be renegotiated.[57] Moreover, the intertextual architecture of the plot, which continuously demands assessment in comparison with Aeschylus's *Oresteia*, is at its core a revision of Aeschylean theology since the possibility of completely domesticating aggressive and bloodthirsty divine forces is rejected, as we have just seen. Divine design is inextricably linked to intertextuality in *Iphigenia among the Taurians*, and to the process of composing tragedy.[58] Euripides himself, as Zeitlin notes, is the author of Athena's ritual prescriptions.[59]

Athena's epiphany comes as a surprise in a play where Artemis or Apollo might more logically be expected to draw events to a close, sibling gods who are patrons of the sibling protagonists.[60] The fourth-century BCE red-figure hydria, which depicts Iphigenia approaching Orestes in front of the Taurian temple, includes images of Apollo and Artemis, but not of Athena, in the upper space of the painting (Fig. 1.3). Athena's appearance, however, ties the drama's conclusion back to Aeschylus's *Eumenides*, where Athena had resolved the issue of Orestes' matricide in the trial of which she reminds us (1469–72). Apollo had been Orestes' champion at that trial, coming to his defence after ordering the crime of matricide. In Euripides, however, Apollo tends to be negatively portrayed. In *Andromache* (1161–5) he is criticized for allowing an ambush and murder to occur in his temple. In *Ion* (436–51) he is reproached for raping young women and abandoning them and their offspring. In *Electra* (1245–6), Apollo's oracular exhortation of matricide is condemned as unwise, and in *Orestes* the god is repeatedly criticized for ordering the matricide and then abandoning his protégé (163–5, 191–3, 285–7, 595–6, 955–6). In *Iphigenia among the Taurians* (103–5), Orestes expresses serious doubts about his patron and Pylades must encourage him to think positively. Unlike Iphigenia, who prays several times to Artemis during the course of the play (1082–8, 1230–3, 1398–402), Orestes never appeals to Apollo, and we have seen in Chapter 2 how the choral song in honour of Apollo presents the god as petulant and greedy for rich offerings. We are left with the mysterious voice that booms out from the Greek ship as it attempts to escape. Is this the voice of Apollo? Once more, we must interpret and infer without being able to say for certain. After Orestes places Iphigenia and the statue of Artemis safely onto the ship, the Messenger reports that 'some voice spoke aloud from the middle of the ship' (1385). The voice exhorts the Greek sailors to take up their oars and start rowing, and says 'we have the things for which we sailed the inhospitable sea and through the Clashing Rocks' (1389–90).

Is it Orestes who makes this rousing speech once on board? That would make sense, but scholars have observed that the anonymity of the voice gives it a supernatural quality, which compares with other miraculous voices reported in Greek tragedy.[6] If the voice does belong to Orestes, moreover, it is strange that the Messenger does not say so since Orestes had been the subject of his previous sentence. The Chorus had imagined that Apollo would accompany the Greek ship on its homeward journey (1128–31). Can we infer that the voice is Apollo's rallying the Greeks for the escape? It is simply impossible to say. In Euripides' *Andromache* (1147–9), a strange and terrible voice speaks forth from the inner shrine of Apollo's temple and rallies a mob to attack Neoptolemus. The voice can only be Apollo's. In *Bacchae* (1078–81), a voice which can only be that of Dionysus is reported urging the maenads to avenge themselves and him on Pentheus. There is no such clarity in *Iphigenia among the Taurians*. Perhaps we are to understand that Orestes has been endowed with this superhuman voice thanks to Apollo, so that god and mortal are conflated in a manner comparable to the conflation of Iphigenia and Artemis. In any case, the efforts to row the ship safely out of reach of the Taurians are thwarted by a new divine intervention. The ship is pushed back to the coast by waves and winds at the mouth of the harbour (1391–5), the work of 'revered Poseidon, ruler of the sea, who watches over Troy and opposes the family of Pelops' (1414–15). As founder and patron of Troy, Poseidon is a natural enemy of the family of Agamemnon whose army had destroyed his city in the Trojan War, and he will only be appeased at Athena's request (1444–5). The intervention of Poseidon underlines the futility of human plans and shows that the gods continue to target humans. In this sense, the gods are 'bad' and Iphigenia's rationalization has been wrong, but that does not mean we should not reflect on Iphigenia's theological arguments. If the gods are indeed all-powerful, then why are they subject to human weaknesses, exaggerated on a divine scale, and how can they condone heinous crimes? The most important conclusion we can draw concerning Euripides' contradictory and elusive presentation of the gods and their rituals in *Iphigenia among the Taurians*, is that he wanted his audience to think about these issues.

Conclusion

Iphigenia among the Taurians is striking both in its proliferation of religious rituals, and in the difficulties the drama poses for any clear interpretation of divine requirements and involvement. Did Agamemnon have a choice in sacrificing Iphigenia? It is fleetingly implied that he did, since the sacrifice was required only in order to launch the expedition. Did Artemis enjoy receiving human sacrifices while they lasted? This cannot be determined for certain, although she will continue to require a symbolic letting of human blood. Will this blood appease the Furies? Presumably so, but this is not made explicit. Is Apollo present to escort the Greek ship? We just don't know. Will Iphigenia welcome her eternal servitude to Artemis? Presumably not wholeheartedly, given her desire to return home at least, even if marriage may no longer be possible for her, but we are not privy to any response on her part. Are the gods brutal or benevolent? The former seems more likely than the latter. Can this really be the way the world works? Euripides' play invites the audience to ponder these serious metaphysical issues precisely by *not* providing any straightforward answers.

5

Reception

The reception history of *Iphigenia among the Taurians* is vast. In her award-winning study of the subject, Edith Hall has demonstrated definitively not only how this drama has inspired multitudinous artistic endeavours from the fourth century BCE to the present day, but also how its plot and subject matter have penetrated deep into the cultural consciousness of the West.[1] From South Italian vase paintings to the history of the Crimea, from the worship of Artemis in antiquity to the development of Modernist aesthetics, and from Roman philosophy to feminism and postcolonialism, and far more besides, Hall leaves no stone unturned in her exposition of the enormous and hitherto unacknowledged inter-cultural influence of this Euripidean play across the globe. In Chapter 1, we observed the influence of the essential plot of *Iphigenia among the Taurians* on subsequent dramatic genres. In this chapter, we will focus on examining how other key issues we have traced in the book have been adapted and manipulated in important ways within the drama's rich reception history. The inter-ethnic relations, male friendship, representations of femininity and religious preoccupations of Euripides' play have all generated remarkable and ideologically specific reincarnations across the millennia.

Inter-ethnic relations

The Black Sea setting and Taurian 'barbarians' of Euripides' *Iphigenia among the Taurians* have often inspired evocations of isolation, desolation and terrifying savages with grisly rituals. It has not been exclusively so, however, and several significant adaptations have represented a more humane side of the Taurians, as Euripides had done. Both aspects are present in one of the earliest surviving explicit re-workings of the raw Euripidean material, namely the exile poetry of Ovid, who was banished from Rome to the coastal Black Sea town of Tomis (modern-day Constanţa in Romania) by the emperor Augustus in 8 CE. The exact nature of Ovid's crime, which he refers to as 'a poem and a mistake' (*Tristia* 2.207), remains unknown, but he would die in exile around ten years later. In *Tristia* 4.4, Ovid refers to his location on 'the cold shores of the Euxine Sea ... called Axenus by men of old' (55–88). Jennifer Ingleheart notes that this is the only use of the term 'Axenus' in Ovid, and that it must be an allusion to the repeated references to the *axenos* 'inhospitable' sea (and land) in Euripides.[2] Ovid thus evokes sympathy for his plight as an exile by implying that Tomis borders on the land of the Taurians, 'who are reported to rejoice in men's blood' (61). In fact, Tomis 'is 739 miles by land, or 212 nautical miles by sea' from the Tauric Chersonese.[3] It is clear that the geographical association is an emotional one exploited to express isolation and suffering. Ovid wishes that, like Orestes, he too might return home 'with the god appeased' (87–8), a hope that he may yet be pardoned by Augustus, whose title *Divi filius* 'son of a god' linked him to the deified Julius Caesar. The poem, which takes the form of a letter, functions like Iphigenia's letter in Euripides. This is the case also in Ovid's later treatment of the myth in one of the poems from his *Letters from the Black Sea* (3.2). Here, once again, Ovid suggests that he is living close to the Taurians (45–6), and goes on to report the events from Euripides' play through a third-party Taurian narrator (48–96). Evidence of the theft of Artemis's statue remains in the form of the empty pedestal that still stands in her temple (51–4). In this case, however, Ovid exploits the Taurian interlocutor to express admiration for the exemplary friendship of Orestes and Pylades, each of whom is willing to die for the other. He is thus able to conclude that, if such virtuous friendship can move even barbarian hearts on the most savage shores, then Romans should be moved by his plight and his friends should come to his aid (99–102).[4] The old Taurian is more enlightened than the Romans on the issue of friendship, to which we shall return below. At the same time, Ovid develops the motif of 'barbarian' admiration for 'Greek' values found in Euripides and gives it a more concrete articulation. Where Thoas had briefly admired Iphigenia's Greek wisdom in Euripides (1180), Ovid's Taurian expresses extended approval for Orestes and Pylades.[5] This type of portrayal is more positive than representations of blood-thirsty savages and dupes, but it remains problematic across the reception history of *Iphigenia among the Taurians* because it validates the customs of the 'aggressor' who has come to steal a valuable native object.

Adaptations in which the barbarian figures are reduced to mere savages work either as comedies or as politicized allegories of fearsome enemies. In the former category is a 'bizarre descendant of [*Iphigenia among the Taurians*]',[6] a burlesque mime from the second century CE set in India with a Greek maiden called Charition in the main role and a cast equivalent to the original play. The Fool (Pylades), Charition (Iphigenia), and Charition's brother (Orestes) plan to escape by serving the Indian King (Thoas) and his men undiluted wine and then tying them up. The performance featured excessive farting, arguments over stealing objects from the goddess's temple where the drama was set, and incomprehensible babbling meant to represent a foreign language.[7] More commonly, however, after the regeneration of interest in Greek tragedy following the Renaissance, the 'barbarians' of the plot are thinly disguised Ottomans. The identification of an Ottoman 'other' is pitted against a Christian 'self' in such adaptations, and we will return to the religious dimension shortly. For now we observe that Ottomanized Taurians are frighteningly and excessively savage. Giovanni Rucellai's 1520s *Oreste* gives his Taurians a complex palace infrastructure and a crowded court reminiscent of the Khans and Sultans of his day. His Toante (Thoas) wishes he could drink human blood and nothing else, and the community as a whole revels in watching blood sports. There is no reconciliation between the Greeks and the Taurians at the end of the play, which concludes with Toante furiously bent on revenge.[8] In the subsequent seventeenth and eighteenth centuries, adaptations of *Iphigenia among the Taurians* were hugely popular both in the theatre and at the opera.[9] One reason for its popularity was the opportunity it afforded for the inclusion of exotic music in the Turkish style.[10] A further common feature in many seventeenth- and eighteenth-century adaptations was the introduction of a love interest sub-plot. Jean Racine had drawn up a plan for the first act of a version of *Iphigenia among the Taurians* in the 1670s but subsequently abandoned the project and never completed it. Significantly, however, Racine had introduced a Taurian prince, son of Thoas, who was in love with Iphigenia. In François Joseph de La Grange-Chancel's 1699 play *Oreste et Pylade*, Thoas becomes king after promising to marry the Taurian king's daughter Thomiris, but Thoas is in love with Iphigenia and wishes to marry her instead, which causes problems. In Gian Rinaldo Carli's 1744 tragedy *Ifigenia in Tauri*, it is Toante's General Fineo who is in love with Ifigenia. In Jean-Baptiste-Claude Vaubertrand's 1757 *Iphigénie en Tauride*, Thoas himself desires Iphigenia's hand.[11] The motif can be traced back to Euripides' *Helen*, which shares a similar plot outline to *Iphigenia among the Taurians*, but where Helen resists the unwanted advances of the Egyptian king.[12] Romantic plots were generally popular in the seventeenth and eighteenth centuries. However, the trope of unwanted advances on Iphigenia also played into the patriarchal fear of Western women being abducted by savage infidels.[13]

In the single most important and influential dramatic adaptation of Euripides' original, Goethe's *Iphigenie auf Tauris*, the Taurian king is in love with Iphigenie. First published in prose form in 1779, and then in verse form in 1787, nineteenth-century illustrations of Goethe's Thoas depict him in Ottoman-style dress (e.g. Fig. 5.1). But this king is both rational and enlightened compared with his recent predecessors. Critics agree that Goethe's drama represents a remarkable moment in the reception history of the play.[14] Goethe's Iphigenie considers Thoas to be 'a noble man' (33, 1864), and he has already ended the custom of human sacrifice under Iphigenie's persuasion. Iphigenie receives praise for this from the king's confidant Arkas. This Arkas is a 'barbarian' with a Greek name meaning 'Arcadian', as Goethe who had studied Greek would well have known.[15] In fact, Racine had used this name for a servant of Agamemnon in his 1674 *Iphigénie* (based on the Aulis myth). In Goethe, Iphigenie's refusal of Thoas's marriage proposal angers him into reintroducing the rites of human sacrifice, just before the arrival of Orest and Pylades. Goethe's Thoas is confused rather than savage. Lonely, and wishing to replace the son he has lost, he has resorted to desiring Iphigenie as a wife, but this is entirely inappropriate to the metaphorical father–daughter relationship that is suggested between them (510–14, 2154–7, cf. 486–71).[16] Goethe's choice of the name Arkas for Thoas's servant, recalling Racine's famous play, may well have been designed to further imply a parallel between Iphigenie's father Agamemnon and Thoas. At the drama's conclusion, moreover, the Greeks and Thoas enter into the very Greek bond of *xenia*, or reciprocal guest-friendship, called 'Gastrecht' in Goethe (2153). Orest realizes the true meaning of Apollo's oracular instruction to retrieve 'the sister' from Tauris (2113). It is Iphigenie rather than Apollo's sister, the statue of Artemis, who must be rescued.

The theft of the foreign treasure is thus abandoned, but the proposed theft is conceptualized by Goethe in colonial terms, as Edith Hall has observed, when Thoas contextualizes it within generalized acts of aggression by Greeks motivated by greed for 'barbarian'

Figure 5.1 Illustration for Goethe's *Iphigenie auf Tauris*. Engraving after a drawing by Ferdinand Rothbart (1823–1899). Thoas, dressed in Ottoman style trousers and slippers and sporting orientalized headgear, speaks with Iphigenia in a grove in front of the Taurian temple of Artemis.

treasures (2102–6). Is the play, then, 'a miracle of cosmopolitan humanism or a sinister crypto-colonial fantasy of domination?'[17] On the former reading, the play celebrates different ethnic groups learning from each other within the context of Enlightenment debates on empire.[18] In this sense, Goethe's play is a direct descendant of John Dennis's *Iphigenia*. Performed in the winter of 1699–1700 for British audiences, Dennis's barbarians, led by a Scythian queen, 'learn from their Grecian visitors to transcend their primitive superstitions and learn the ways of the Enlightenment gentleman'.[19] On the latter reading, however, Goethe's drama represents 'a fantasy of imposing a new moral order . . . in which backward peoples *consent* to have their ritual practices and values dictated by more advanced ones'.[20] Again, we can compare Dennis, whose Scythian queen willingly hands over rule of her empire to the Greeks, and whose drama is a clear attempt to justify British colonialism.[21]

Postcolonial readings of Goethe's *Iphigenie* have dominated scholarship since the 1960s. The play was a staple of the German theatre under the Nazi regime, and has been identified as an aesthetically disguised racist endorsement of German nationalism and imperialism.[22] At the same time, the atrocities committed by the Nazis have been associated with a truly barbaric version of the Taurians. *The Pathseeker*, a 2008 novel by Imre Kertész, originally published in Hungarian in 1977, suggests that Goethe's version of events disguises what really happened. In fact, Orestes and Pylades were attacked by the Taurian soldiers, subdued, shackled, made to watch the Taurians rape Iphigenia, and were then hacked to pieces in front of her. Iphigenia, already desensitized to such horrors, is dispatched, and the Taurians take off to the theatre for the evening to watch Thoas being clement on stage as they snigger up their sleeves. The experience of Holocaust victims is thus '"ventriloquized" through . . . a conversation about classical tragedy.'[23] Goethe, of course, could not have foreseen the rise of the Third Reich, and for all the patronizing crypto-colonial sentiment and improbable psychologies in his *Iphigenie*, there is no doubt that his drama represents a new take on inter-ethnic relationships.

Remarkably, the year 1779 saw the production of the two most influential adaptations of *Iphigenia among the Taurians*. As Goethe's prose version of *Iphigenie* first came into being, so too did Gluck's opera *Iphigénie en Tauride*. The libretto for Gluck's opera, by Nicolas-François Guillard, was based on the 1757 dramatic version of Claude Guimond de La Touche with some significant adaptations, such as the reintroduction of the Chorus and the *dea ex machina*.[24] Interestingly, Guimond de La Touche had gone against contemporary practice by removing the romantic episode in the final version of his play.[25] Nevertheless, the plot follows a straightforwardly negative portrayal of the Taurians. They are eager for the blood sacrifice of the Greeks to take place. Thoas is killed by Pylades and the Greeks are about to rout the Scythians in the final act when the goddess Diana appears and orders the Scythians to return her statue to Greece. It seems clear, however, that Thoas in de La Touche's play was meant to represent Louis XV who had become unpopular in France from the mid-eighteenth century and had died in 1774.[26] Cruelty and tyranny, the parallel implies, had become home-grown, and the crisis of public opposition to the monarchy would gather momentum until the French Revolution was unleashed in 1789. In Gluck, it was music that enabled the opera to 'become an icon of a broader revolutionary vector in Paris.'[27] The opera itself was revolutionary in musical terms for rejecting the kind of ostentation, particularly of vocal display, that had become standard in eighteenth-century opera. Gluck rather promoted an economy of form and a prioritizing of emotional effect that he perceived as a return to the principles of Greek tragedy.[28] In line with this approach, Gluck's opera reasserts the importance of the Chorus, making their presence integral to the action. The Chorus of Greek priestesses that attend Iphigenia is supplemented by a Chorus of Scythians, and the ethnicity of each is stressed through their music. The Scythian ballet 'is raucous and savage, perfectly contrasting with the tranquility and amplitude of the rather often liturgical music sung by the Greek priestesses.'[29] Gluck's Thoas is also characterized through orientalizing musical effects.[30] In Pina Bausch's choreography for her 1974 dance opera, *Iphigenie auf Tauris*, inspired by Gluck, the Greek males Orestes and Pylades possess 'interior and spiritual freedom' represented by the naked body, while Thoas is emotionally constrained by a heavy costume. Ethnicity thus becomes politicized through dance.[31]

Emphasizing the ethnic 'otherness' of Thoas and the Taurians continued to be a significant aspect of major adaptations of Euripides' original. The early twentieth-century production directed by Harley Granville-Barker, using the recent translation of Gilbert Murray and starring Lillah McCarthy, made lavish use of orientalizing costumes. First performed in London in 1912, the production toured North America in 1915 to massive audiences in university sports stadia. The costumes for the barbarian characters, however, which were garish and flamboyant, drew many negative responses and even ridicule from reviewers, for whom they represented caricatures of the Arab world or of African tribes.[32] Edith Hall has suggested that the Taurian 'savages' of Granville-Barker's production, who are taught a higher truth thanks to the Greeks, evoke imperial and missionary endeavours in Africa. Hall further develops Levi Post's identification of *Iphigenia among the Taurians* as the Ur-text underlying the 1927 bestseller *Trader Horn*, in which a British girl held captive by a savage African tribe escapes thanks to a an ivory trader and his best friend. Hall shows how the film version of *Trader Horn*, produced in 1931, influenced a whole new genre of adventure movies, beginning with *Tarzan* in 1932. Palpably racist in their representation of non-whites, such films were nevertheless hugely popular with contemporary audiences, thus demonstrating how deeply Euripides' plot had penetrated into Western culture, albeit in distorted form.[33]

In Latin America, early twentieth-century colonial ideology manifests itself rather differently in the 1923 *Ifigenia Cruel* by Mexican author Alfonso Reyes. Ifigenia has forgotten her original identity and is aware only of her duty to kill human victims in honour of Artemis (a task which she carries out herself). When Orestes realizes who she is, he makes her remember her past, but she is so horrified by the crimes of her family that she refuses to return with him to Greece and chooses to remain among the Taurians and continue her grisly duties. Toas shows clemency and allows the Greeks to leave, but Orestes must return to Greece empty-handed, having failed in his mission. The play has challenged interpreters because Ifigenia is at once liberated by her choice, but also simultaneously 'reborn a slave' to the goddess.[34] As a well-travelled Mexican, Reyes had a complex 'sense of ethnic and cultural hybridity', which must have informed his remarkable adaptation of the play.[35] In his version, the rites of human sacrifice echo ancient Aztec culture, to which Ifigenia has become assimilated, and the colonial agenda fails when the Greeks are expelled without the prize they had come to seek. A similar conflation of indigenous and colonial experiences features in Louis Nowra's 1985 *The Golden Age*, set in the Tasmanian wilderness. It tells the story of a strange community discovered just before World War II, who are descended from deported nineteenth-century convicts. In its isolation, the group has developed its own dialect and cultural practices. Like Reyes's Ifigenia, the community represents aspects of both indigenous tribes and colonial settlement. Nowra's drama is framed by two productions of *Iphigenia among the Taurians*, which represent a colonial effort to impose a European 'high' culture into the new world. At the same time, the Euripidean plot is loosely re-worked through the main action. Two close male friends (Francis and Peter) discover the lost 'tribe' and try unsuccessfully to reintegrate them into society. All members of the group end up dying, mostly of tuberculosis, except for Betsheb, who functions as an Iphigenia figure. Francis acknowledges that he and the Australian government have destroyed the tribe, and takes Betsheb back to the Tasmanian wilderness electing to live with her there. The play has been called 'the most comprehensively counter-imperial text in Australian theatre'.[36]

We have come a long way from Euripides, both conceptually and geographically. Nevertheless, the diversity of ethnically charged responses to the raw material demonstrates the potential for the original to be read and developed in strikingly different ways, ranging from the farcical effects of burlesqued or ridiculously costumed foreigners to the serious and disturbing promotion of an imperialist agenda or a radical rejection thereof.

Gender dynamics

Gender issues are central to *Iphigenia among the Taurians*, as we have seen, but many of the responses to the drama have placed rather different emphases on issues of masculinity or femininity. The two young men at the heart of the adventure plot, Orestes and Pylades, have generated their own rather independent strand of existence as models for idealized male friendship within the play's reception history. The Romans, in particular, seem to have greatly admired how each man each is willing to stay and die so that the other can live, when one of them is given the opportunity to go back to Greece, while the other must stay to be sacrificed to Artemis/Diana. The first-century BCE philosopher Cicero, in his treatise *On Friendship* (7.24) refers to a theatrical scene in which each man tries to die for the other, which led to rapturous applause from the audience. The play in question was by Marcus Pacuvius, working in the second century BCE, and is regrettably lost to us, but it was very clearly an adaptation of the original by Euripides.[37] As Edith Hall has observed, the Roman concept of friendship, *amicitia*, valued symmetry of class, age and life experience. This made it quite different from the Greek *philia*, which was a bond of friendship that could exist across far more varied social and kinship lines. Competition was also important in Roman notions of ideal friendship so that the contest of self-sacrifice staged between Orestes and Pylades in the land of the Taurians was a significant element in its appeal.[38] The contest is repeated in Ovid (*Letters from the Black Sea* 3.2.85–9). Like Pacuvius before him, Ovid removes Pylades' non-altruistic motivation. In Euripides, Pylades fears that his reputation would suffer if he were to return to Greece alone and says that he should stay and die together with Orestes, but later accepts Orestes' request to go back with the letter (578–717). Jennifer Ingleheart notes that Ovid emphasizes instead 'the mutual love of the young heroes', a motif which is specifically indebted to Roman tragedy.[39]

The relationship between Orestes and Pylades continued to fascinate intellectuals writing under the Roman empire. The Syrian author Lucian, working in the second century CE, references the two men in the opening of his dialogue on friendship *Toxaris*. In this dialogue, a Greek, Mnesippus, and a Scythian Toxaris (meaning 'Archer' in Greek), decide to embark on a story-telling competition to demonstrate the excellence of Greek and Scythian friends, respectively, and end up becoming friends themselves by the end of the dialogue.[40] Toxaris suggests that the Scythians are better than the Greeks at admiring heroic exempla since Orestes and Pylades are worshipped in Scythia for their extraordinary loyalty, even though they are foreigners (5–6). Lucian's text repeats the trope of the admiring barbarian introduced by Ovid through his Taurian narrator, and also employed by Goethe. Interestingly, however, Toxaris stresses the reciprocity of action in the behaviour of Orestes and Pylades, showing the influence of Roman thought. Each man in Lucian's account tries to protect the other from blows and attacks, thus developing the one-sided Euripidean paradigm where it was Pylades who had protected a vulnerable Orestes from attack. That attack, during Orestes' fit of madness, is alluded to specifically in another work attributed to Lucian (*Erotes* 47), where the relationship between the men is presented as an erotic one. The scene from Euripides, in which Pylades holds up his cloak to shield Orestes, is used to illustrate that Pylades behaves as a lover would. Among Christians in antiquity, the friendship of Orestes and Pylades continued to be evoked as model. In his *Confessions* (4.6), Augustine ponders the loss of his dear friend and considers that he would not have been willing to die in his place, unlike Orestes and Pylades, a passage which has led to a bitter controversy over Augustine's possible early homosexual experiences and their implications for the teachings of Christianity on this subject.[41] In later Christianizing readings, one man's desire to sacrifice himself for the sake of others could take on martyrological aspects, such as Rucellai's Oreste who is 'almost Christ-like' in his willingness to die and is unafraid of death, safe in the knowledge that his soul will be returned to God after death.[42]

The philosophical or metaphysical focus on the existential value of the type of male friendship exemplified in the experiences of Orestes and Pylades inevitably entailed the erasure of Iphigenia from view. When she reappears in theatrical or operatic adaptations, she is often cast against the sentimentalized friendship of Orestes and Pylades whose prominence has been developed. John Dennis's *Iphigenia* (1700) refers to Cicero's treatise *On Friendship* in an inscription beneath his play's title, and presents the two friends overcoming the superstitious Scythians through their superior intellect and values.[43] The shift in focus is evident from titles such as François Joseph de La Grange-Chancel's *Oreste et Pylade* (1699) and Johann Elias Schlegel's *Orest und Pylades* (1737). Both present a confrontation between the Greek men and Thoas in which each man vies altruistically to be Thoas's target.[44] Schlegel, arguably for the first time before Goethe, emphasizes Iphigenia's gender.[45] Thoas has previously ridiculed her as helpless, Iphigenia reports, but now he will see that she, as a woman, will vanquish him through deception and trickery (Act 4, Scene 4). Goethe's development of gender dynamics, however, is radically new, and his Iphigenia is sympathetic in a way that previous Iphigenias often were not.[46] Iphigenia had been ennobled by John Dennis in his *Iphigenia* of 1700, and Guimond de La Touche had emphasized Iphigenia's humanity in 1757. It was Goethe, however, who explicitly connected his Iphigenie's humanity with her femininity.

Goethe's powerful thematization of gender can be traced to Euripides, but it is informed by contemporary values and turn of the eighteenth century norms. In Iphigenie's opening speech, she laments the plight of women stressing that even obeying a harsh husband is duty and consolation rather than being driven to distant lands (23–34). This reflects views of the male educated elite for whom women should be gentle and loving consorts for their husbands and uphold moral standards in the family home.[47] It represented a new kind of femininity where the ideal woman was responsible for the private sphere of human values, as opposed to the previously idealized 'Hausmutter' whose role was to labour constantly on the farm.[48] Man is master, both at home and abroad, claims Iphigenie (25–6), but the play validates Iphigenie's feminine morals while the masculine way of brute force is questioned and found wanting. When Iphigenie turns down Thoas's marriage proposal and explains that she wishes to return home, the king flies into a rage. In a misogynistic rant he tells Iphigenie to be 'just like a woman' in abandoning herself to unrestrained desire. 'When passion burns in women's bosoms,' Thoas continues, 'no sacred bond restrains them from the traitor who entices them from the long since reliable arms of father and husband; and when the rapid heat is calmed in her breast then the golden tongue of persuasion pushes its own way through powerfully and with vain loyalty' (468–74). Thoas's accusations are all completely unfounded in Iphigenie's case, and his mention of 'father and husband' illustrates his confusion over the nature of his relationship with Iphigenie that we noted above. Goethe's Iphigenie is idealized, in part, by her chastity, but also by her feminine ability to persuade which is divorced from the negative connotations of deception in Goethe. Iphigenie will ultimately achieve her goal through persuasion, yes, but also through love, and kindness, and honesty.

Iphigenie is the only female character in Goethe. He does not introduce an additional confidante or Taurian princess, as others had often done, and he dispenses entirely with the Chorus. This underlines Iphigenie's isolation, but it also sharpens the contrast between gendered approaches to the problems in Tauris. Men are associated with physical violence in the play, and with cruelty. Pylades, for example, comments that it is to their advantage that Iphigenie is a woman since even the best of men will become accustomed to cruelty, while a woman will remain constant in her (benevolent) disposition (786–93). Responding to Thoas's rant, Iphigenie had replied 'O King, do not scold our poor sex. It is not glorious like yours, but neither are a woman's weapons ignoble. Believe what I predict for you in this matter, that I know your fortune better than yourself' (481–5). Herein lies the key to Goethe's representation of gender. The male is heroic, driven to action, but the female, as represented by Iphigenie and the religious authority bestowed on her, is divinely inspired.[49] As a human character, Goethe's Iphigenie may well be 'psychologically implausible'.[50] Her lack of rancour against the father who sacrificed her, for example, is improbable in real terms.[51] But this Iphigenie does not represent a *real* woman. She is highly idealized through Christianizing language, as we shall discuss further below, and also aesthetically through her function as a substitute for the statue of Diana. Writing in the mid-eighteenth century, Johann Joachim Winckelmann had an enormous influence on German thinkers.[52] Winckelmann propounded the association of classical Greece with nature, beauty and freedom in contrast to the contemporary baroque world which was shown to be unnatural and corrupt. Winckelmann was primarily concerned with the visual arts, including sculpture, in his theorization of aesthetic ideals. It is within this framework that we should understand the remarkable claim made by Goethe's Iphigenie that she 'was born as free as a man' (1858). To a modern audience, this suggestion seems incompatible with Iphigenie's previous assertions of male authority and female subservience, but the freedom to which Iphigenie refers must be understood in philosophical terms. Nicholas Boyle notes that Goethe was indebted to the theories of human freedom put forward by the seventeenth-century Dutch philosopher Baruch Spinoza.[53] Spinoza rejected the notion of free will, but connected human freedom with the ability to understand why we behave the way we do through concentration on the divine. As the most insightful of the characters, who is associated with the divine, Iphigenie can claim freedom on these terms. Aesthetically, however, Iphigenie may also be associated with freedom, as well as with nature and with beauty, in order to embody the contemporary projection of Winckelmann's statuesque Greek ideal.

Greek sculpture would inspire the representation of Iphigenia more directly in Granville-Barker's early-twentieth-century touring production, where Lillah McCarthy's costume in the first part of the play was based on the iconography of the archaic Greek *korai* statues.[54] These free-standing statues of *korai* 'maidens', many of which have been found at the Acropolis in Athens, date from the sixth and early fifth centuries BCE. They are characterized by a rigid posture, a restrained 'smile', heavily draped robes and stiffly braided hair. It took the art of modern dance, however, to release, finally, a feminist response to the rich raw material of the Taurian legend. Inspired by Gluck's Iphigenia operas, pioneering dance innovator Isadora Duncan choreographed twenty dances based on the Iphigenia story between 1903 and 1916. In Greek tragedy, Duncan found expression, ritual and the Chorus, all of which were essential to her conception of the function of dance. Duncan's dances were based primarily on choral episodes, not characters, and her interpretation of Taurian Iphigenia was informed by Gluck's 'Dance of the Scythians'. Duncan's Iphigenia was Amazonian in celebrating victory over enemies and dragging victims to their deaths.[55] Her portrayal of Iphigenia can be linked to her belief in the emancipation of women, as Alessandra Zanobi observes. Zanobi further suggests that Duncan's Iphigenia shares 'Goethe's concept of the eternal feminine'.[56] As an early feminist, however, Duncan's Iphigenia, who embraces violence, is also radically different from Goethe's since the latter rejects it utterly and remains circumscribed within a traditional patriarchal culture. Influenced by Duncan, Pina Bausch's 1974 dance drama *Iphigenie auf Tauris* is also concerned with the feminine but is not overtly feminist. Rather, Bausch went so far as to deny being a feminist and extended the theme of sacrifice to both genders in her work.[57]

Feminist adaptations of *Iphigenia among the Taurians* are not as common as one might expect given the potential of the original. Two US productions from the 1990s stressed issues of female oppression in patriarchal societies through the myth of Taurian Iphigenia. Ellen McLaughlin's *Iphigenia and Other Daughters*, which premiered in New York in 1995, used material from Euripides' two Iphigenia plays to frame a version of Sophocles' *Electra*. Iphigenia is the object of the male gaze both on the point of being sacrificed at the opening of the play, and in the drama's conclusion where she becomes the statue that Orestes must return to Greece. McLaughlin thus exploits the conflation of Artemis and Iphigenia evoked in the original, and more fully developed by Goethe. In casting Iphigenia as the object of the male gaze at the moment of her sacrifice, she may also have been inspired by Aeschylus's description of the sacrifice where Iphigenia 'stands out as if in a painting' (*Ag.* 241–2) while the warriors of the Greek army look on. Helene Foley discusses how, although Iphigenia remains 'the object of the fascinated male gaze, she turned from victim to a source of salvation at the center of history' by the end of the play. This ending 'attempts to include both history and familial bonds, both the personal and the political so central to contemporary feminism at the time of the first performance of McLaughlin's play, yet recognizes the largely symbolic nature of its conclusion.'[58] JoAnne Akalaitis' *The Iphigenia Cycle*, first performed in Chicago in 1997 and revived in New York in 1999, also combines Euripides' two Iphigenia tragedies. As a director for whom 'classical drama can play a vital role in the struggle against all forms of oppression, patriarchy included',[59] Akalaitis stressed the victimization and sufferings of women who become 'trapped by an absurd, deadly, and sometimes laughable male war game'.[60] Following in a similar vein, Iphigenia's victimization was emphasized once more through the framing device of her sacrifice at Aulis in Classics Professor Mary-Kay Gamel's 2010 *Effie and the Barbarians*, performed in Philadelphia.[61]

The same year, in Michi Barall's 2010 tragicomic and self-conscious *Rescue Me (A Postmodern Classic with Snacks)*, which premiered in Ohio, a contemporary Iphigenia, approaching her mid–30s, is single with real-life problems. She hates her job and knows her chances of becoming a mother are diminishing, but she is also a psychologically insightful character, which gives her an edge over the men in the play. Edith Hall examines how the feminist concerns of this adaptation have 'palpably evolved'. Iphigenia's desire to become a wife and mother is thoroughly acceptable and her problem is 'less that she hates her job than that she has no emotional life'.[62] In fact, this is a remarkably accurate updating of the original Iphigenia's plight, who deeply laments her unmarried and childless status and detests her duties in the cult of Taurian Artemis. Barall's Iphigenia refuses Thoas's offer of marriage, a motif adapted from Goethe though in this case the proposal is made to seem reasonable. This thoroughly modern and independent Iphigenia, however, clearly does not wish to 'settle' for a suitor she feels is not right for her, even if he is not such a bad guy.

Gender roles are further complicated in the play through the introduction of the goddess Artemis acted by a man dressed in an impressive business suit, implicitly reminding the audience that all female roles in Greek drama were played by men.[63] The most recent adaptation of *Iphigenia among the Taurians* goes even further in this regard. Tony Harrison's verse drama *Iphigenia in Crimea* premiered on BBC Radio 3 on 20th April 2017. Set during the Crimean War of the mid-nineteenth century, it features a Classics-trained British lieutenant, stationed at Sevastopol in 1854, who has been reading *Iphigenia among the Taurians*. He is aware that the drama was set in the vicinity, in the ancient city of Chersonesos, and persuades his men to perform the play 'to lighten spirits in the bleak Crimea'. The men dress in drag, creating costumes from clothes taken from an abandoned aristocrat's house. But there is a serious point being made in inserting this play into a context of warfare since the original is about the aftermath of a huge war, the Trojan War, as Harrison observes.[64] Where contemporary adaptations of more obvious Greek war plays, like Euripides' *Trojan Women* or Sophocles' *Ajax*, explicitly assert the value of Greek drama as an antidote or a kind of therapy for the psychological trauma of warfare,[65] Harrison's *Iphigenia in Crimea* expresses this implicitly.

Religion

The absence of Artemis from the conclusion of *Iphigenia among the Taurians* prevents a straightforward conclusion regarding the goddess's views on the practice of human sacrifice in her honour, as we discussed in the last chapter, although the continued requirement for the shedding of human blood demonstrates that the she does require at least a symbolic offering. Subsequent treatments tend to elide these ambiguities. In Ovid, for example, Iphigenia happily carries off the statue of the goddess 'who hated cruel rites', bringing her to a better place (*Tristia* 4.4.80–1). The Euripidean Iphigenia's concerns over the theft of the statue and the implications of a continued requirement of human bloodshed are no longer an issue. Far more striking, however, in terms of Roman religious appropriation of the myth, is the frequent appearance of Iphigenia, Orestes and Pylades depicted in front of the Taurian temple on Roman sarcophagi (e.g. Fig. 5.2). Drawing on work by Ruth Bielfeldt, Edith Hall has explained why this trio and this episode were so popular in Roman funerary art. The two young men, as we have discussed, were a model for the Roman ideal of friendship (*amicitia*), and their presence in a sacred

Figure 5.2 Detail from a Roman sarcophagus, *c.* 140 CE, depicting a scene related to Euripides' *Iphigenia among the Taurians*. Glyptothek, Munich, Germany. Iphigenia holds the statue of Artemis (on the right). Behind her stands a Taurian attendant holding a flaming torch and a catapult (presumably a reference to the Taurians who pelted Orestes and Pylades with stones in Euripides' play). His gaze is directed towards Pylades who leans forward to support a seated and suffering Orestes. Framed by these two figures, Orestes is the focus of the scene. Behind Pylades stands a Taurian wearing the distinctive 'barbarian' hat.

space controlled by the priestess Iphigenia as they consider imminent death can be read as a display of another Roman virtue, *pietas* (a piety defined by duty). The kinship between the three figures would also have resonated with familial loss.[66]

Since the Renaissance, on the other hand, apart from the exploration of the ritual dimension of Greek tragedy in the creation of modern dance by Isadora Duncan and Pina Bausch, most responses to *Iphigenia among the Taurians*, which include a religious dimension, have inserted a Christianizing element into the narrative.[67] Rucellai's 1520s Iphigenia, for example, is a 'thinly disguised Roman Catholic nun dedicated to the Virgin Mary'.[68] In an entirely different context, John Dennis's 1700 Greeks are cultured and rational in the face of superstitious Scythians in an overtly anti-Jacobite (and so anti-Catholic) production. Cast against persecutions and executions of Whigs from the 1680s, the savage practices of the Taurians were obviously allegorical, and since contemporary politics were entirely tied up with issues of religion, Dennis's interpretation has religious implications. In terms of plot, however, he stripped away most of the divine elements, including the *dea ex machina* and many of the references to divine intervention, as had La Grange-Chancel in his *Oreste et Pylade* (1699). Dennis even does away with Iphigenia's sacrifice. Agamemnon did not sacrifice his daughter in this version but was the one who smuggled her to safety in a ship. The Greeks are thus entirely rehabilitated.[69] This paring down of divine intrusions was common in theatrical adaptations but not at the opera, which delighted in the spectacular effects of a divine epiphany. Gluck even introduced the Furies on stage tormenting Orestes in Act 2. In Gluck, as elsewhere, however, the concluding epiphany is not of Athena, but of Diana.[70] In this way, the goddess's own wishes are made clear. She directly commands the end of gruesome violence in her honour and the ambiguities that remained in the original are once again removed.

Goethe's play, like those of his dramatic predecessors, dispensed with any divine epiphany from the drama's conclusion.[71] At the same time, however, his *Iphigenie* is heavily laced through with Christian imagery. Although Goethe himself subscribed to a doctrine of classical humanism, rather than to either of the dominant Catholic or Protestant religions, and read the Bible with a critical mind, the Bible remained the 'main focus of his religious awareness' and 'the main source of his moral education'.[72] His Iphigenie is an 'ideal' in large part because she is characterized through Christianizing language of purity and holiness. She is addressed as 'holy virgin' (65), aligning her with the Virgin Mary, and is repeatedly called 'holy' throughout the drama. Iphigenie has a divine force for healing (*heilig* 'holy' and *heilen* 'to heal' are cognates in German). Orest will claim that he was touched by Iphigenie and was healed (2119–20), and that evil grasped him for the last time and then fled like a serpent to its lair (2124). Iphigenie offers the gods 'a pure heart and incense and prayer' (774). She has a pure hand and a pure heart (1701, 1968). By rejecting deceit Iphigenie will achieve the redemption of her house.[73] As we noticed above, Goethe's presentation of Iphigenie is a significant moment in the gender politics of the play's reception history. It is through the divine aspect of her femininity, however, that she is able to exert a conciliatory and non-threatening power over the male characters.

Among more recent adaptations, only a small number allude to religious issues. 'The Return of Iphigenia', a poetic soliloquy published by the Greek socialist poet Yannis Ritsos in his 1972 collection *The Fourth Dimension*, implicitly links the tyranny of the ruling Greek military Junta with the power of the Greek Orthodox Church. There are no ethnically distinguished foreigners in this work, rather the barbarians are sinister government officials.[74] In the experimental *Ifigenia w Taurydzie*, produced near Lublin in Poland in 2011 by the Centre for Theatre Practices 'Gardzienice', different images of statues of Artemis were exploited alongside rituals still performed in honour of Poland's Black Madonna of Częstochowa. The production thus created a powerful parallel between pagan and Christian symbols in a manner which, as Edith Hall points out, recalls the same suggestion made in 1772 by Voltaire to Catherine the Great, herself an admirer of *Iphigenia among the Taurians*, as she contemplated the conquest and Christianization of the Ottoman Crimea, which she had successfully annexed by 1783.[75]

Conclusion

The reception history of *Iphigenia among the Taurians* demonstrates beyond question the power of this play to address a huge range of issues central to the human condition. The ambiguities of Euripides' original actively encourage new interpretations of the play's central preoccupations with inter-ethnic relations, gender roles in society, and questions of religious or metaphysical piety. On all three of these themes, Goethe's *Iphigenie auf Tauris* has been identified as contributing something new, and is easily the most influential of all adaptations of the play. However, it must also be emphasized that Goethe's apparent innovations are rooted in a close reading of the original. Like Gluck, who must take second place, if not joint first, as a landmark adaptation of the drama, Goethe goes back to Euripides and to Greek tragedy itself for inspiration. The latent politics of the original, moreover, have found concrete and developed expression in many re-workings of the play, which have exposed the ugliness of colonialism, the patriarchal victimization of women, and 'a confrontation with both personal and national identity',[76] whether in terms of ethnicity, gender or religious belief.

Glossary of Greek and Technical Terms

aeolo-choriambic a distinctive metre used by the lyric poets of the eastern Aegean
aition the cause of something explained through myth (hence an aetiology)
anagnōrisis recognition, required along with *peripateia* for the best kind of tragic plot, according to Aristotle
anapaests chanted metrical units used to announce slow entries
antilabai an exchange in which each character speaks half a line in turn
arkteia a religious festival 'of the bears' for girls performed in honour of Artemis
axenos inhospitable
choes individual beakers used for drinking wine at the eponymous *Choes* festival in honour of Dionysus
deictic pronouns pronouns with a fixed point of reference
dithyramb a song accompanied by a circular dance performed competitively by Choruses of men and boys
dochmiac a lyric metre used to express heightened emotion
iambic trimetre the metre used in Greek tragedy for speech and dialogue (as opposed to song)
katabasis a heroic quest to descend to the Underworld
kyrios a male guardian required by all Athenian citizen women (with the possible exception of priestesses)
mēchanē a stage crane (literally a 'contrivance' or 'machine') used in Greek theatre to 'fly in' characters (normally divinities)
metabolē reversal, referring to the overall reversal of events containing *anagnōrisis* and *peripateia* preferred by Aristotle
nomos law or custom
parodos the opening song of the Chorus
peripeteia reversal of fortune, required along with *anagnōrisis* for the best kind of tragic plot, according to Aristotle
Pythia priestess of Apollo's oracular shrine at Delphi

stasimon a choral song subsequent to the *parodos*
stichomythia line-by-line exchange of dialogue between two characters
xenia the Greek concept of reciprocal guest friendship
xenos (plural **xenoi**) can mean 'host', 'guest' or 'stranger'

Guide to Further Reading

The past few years have generated exciting and important new work on *Iphigenia among the Taurians*. The exquisite 2014 translation by poet and Classicist Anne Carson is an ideal starting point. At the same time, the excellent 1999 prose translation by the late Classics scholar and theatre expert James Morwood remains valuable. Two new editions and commentaries on the Greek text have recently been published. Laetitia Parker's 2016 edition gives copious literal translations in its commentary and is an authoritative point of departure on issues of grammar, textual criticism and metre. For French readers, the 2017 edition of Christine and Luc Amiech provides a detailed and useful commentary and a facing French translation. These two new editions complement that of Martin Cropp from 2000, which continues to be an excellent guide on a broad range of thematic and textual issues handled with a light touch. Cropp's edition, like that of David Kovacs, is published with a facing English translation of the Greek text. Part of the Loeb Classical Library series, Kovacs's 1999 edition is necessarily constrained by the series' commitment to brevity in the accompanying introduction and notes. For the more technically advanced reader, who does not require translations of Greek words or phrases, Poulheria Kyriakou's 2006 English commentary contains a wealth of information keyed to James Diggle's 1981 edition of the Greek text.

It is impossible to appreciate *Iphigenia among the Taurians* fully without some knowledge of Greek religious practices. Burkert (1985) is still useful and authoritative on the subject, but Robert Parker (2005 and 2011) has done much to further develop our understanding of classical Greek religion. On the connections between Greek tragedy and religion, Christiane Sourvinou-Inwood (2003) proposes a deep symbiosis, while others, such as Scott Scullion (2002 and 2005), have rejected the notion that tragedy should be conceived as a ritual in itself. Scullion (2000) has also suggested that ritual aetiologies, of the kind we find in *Iphigenia among the Taurians*, are largely the poet's invention, while Richard Seaford (2009) maintains that they must be based to a large extent on lived experiences in order to make sense. The question of whether or not Iphigenia was worshipped at Brauron remains hotly contested, but Gunnel Ekroth (2003) gives a detailed analysis concluding that this was unlikely. Christian Wolff (1992), Angeliki Tzanetou (2000), and Thalia Papadopoulou (2005b), meanwhile, have read the rituals described by the play within the immediate dramatic context in illuminating ways. David Sansone's 1975 analysis of the sacrifice motif in *Iphigenia among the Taurians* also remains valuable.

On the theme of escape, and on issues of philosophical and metaphysical debate, Matthew Wright (2005) is authoritative, and on the inter-textual engagement of *Iphigenia among the Taurians* with the *Oresteia*, the work of Froma Zeitlin (2005 and 2011) is characteristically enlightening. The most important study of the play, however, is Edith Hall's 2013 *Adventures with Iphigenia*. This extraordinarily detailed cultural history guides the reader through the reception of the play from the fifth century BCE to the twenty-first century CE. Hall pays particular attention to issues of performance in the play's reception history, to the importance of the worship of Artemis in antiquity, and to the social and political climates that generated each new interpretation of the play. For a briefer but nevertheless helpful overview of the drama's reception, Mills (2015) can also be warmly recommended.

Selected Chronology

BCE

490–479	Persian Wars
458	Aeschylus's *Oresteia* produced
455	Euripides' first attested dramatic production
431–404	Peloponnesian War
415	Euripides, *Trojan Women*
c. 414	Euripides, *Iphigenia among the Taurians*
412	Euripides, *Helen*
second century	Marcus Pacuvius produces a Roman tragedy based on the Taurian myth
44	Cicero, *De Amicitia*

CE

c. 8–17	Ovid, *Tristia* and *Letters from the Black Sea*
c. 163	Lucian, *Toxaris*
second century	*Chariton* mime
fourth century	*Erotes*, attributed to Lucian
397–400	Augustine, *Confessions*
1520s	Giovanni Rucellai, *Oreste*
1670s	Jean Racine drafts the first act for an adaptation of *Iphigenia among the Taurians* (but abandons the project)
1699	François Joseph de La Grange-Chancel, *Oreste et Pylade*
1699–1700	John Dennis, *Iphigenia*
1737	Johann Elias Schlegel, *Orest und Pylades*
1744	Gian Rinaldo Carli, *Ifigenia in Tauri*
1757	Claude Guimond de la Touche, *Iphigénie en Tauride*

1757	Jean-Baptiste-Claude Vaubertrand, *Iphigénie en Tauride*
1779	Johann Wolfgang von Goethe, *Iphigenie auf Tauris* (prose version)
	Christoph Willibald Gluck, *Iphigénie en Tauride*
1787	Johann Wolfgang von Goethe, *Iphigenie auf Tauris* (verse version)
1903–1916	Isadora Duncan choreographs dances based on Gluck's *Iphigénie en Tauride*
1912	London production of Harley Granville-Barker's *Iphigenia in Tauris*, using the translation of Gilbert Murray
1915	North American tour of Granville-Barker's 1912 production
1923	Alfonso Reyes, *Ifigenia Cruel*
1927	Ethelreda Lewis and Aloysuis Horn, *Trader Horn*
1972	Yannis Ritsos, 'The Return of Iphigenia'
1974	Pina Bausch, *Iphigenie auf Tauris*
1977	Imre Kertész, *The Pathseeker* (English translation, 2008)
1985	Louis Nowra, *The Golden Age*
1995	Ellen McLaughlin, *Iphigenia and Other Daughters*
1997	JoAnne Akalaitis, *The Iphigenia Cycle*
2010	Michi Barall, *Rescue Me (A Postmodern Classics with Snacks)*
	Mary-Kay Gamel, *Effie and the Barbarians*
2011	Centre for Theatre Practices 'Gardzienice', *Ifigenia w Taurydzie*
2017	Tony Harrison, *Iphigenia in Crimea*

Notes

1 Setting, Action, Plot

1. Wright 2005 and 2006.
2. On the metrical qualities of the ancient Greek language, see D'Angour 2009.
3. For more detailed discussion of the dating of *Iphigenia among the Taurians*, see especially L. Parker 2016: lxxvi–lxxx, with further references.
4. See Braund 1994: 124–5, and Hall 2013: 61.
5. See further Goff 2009: 27–35.
6. Goff 2004: 341. On the theme of salvation in *Iphigenia among the Taurians*, see also Burnett 1971: 47–8, and Hall 2013: 27–8 who connects the rescue theme with worship of Artemis the 'Saviour'.
7. See further Hall 2013: 59–60.
8. For further discussion of the Greek conception of the Black Sea in the classical period, see West 2003.
9. On the selective, but reliable presentation of Black Sea geography by Euripides in this play, see Hall 1987.
10. On the likelihood of a display emphasizing human sacrifice on this stage building, see Torrance 2009.
11. For a detailed discussion of vase paintings featuring scenes from *Iphigenia among the Taurians*, many of which come from southern Italy and attest to the popularity of Euripides' play there, see Hall 2013: 69–91.
12. Garland 1990: 77 notes that 'the most striking feature of Athenian priests and priestesses is their isolation'.
13. Burkert 1985: 94 with 385 n. 110 observes the example of Iphigenia living in the temple as an exception to the norm. See Chapter 4 on the cult statue and on Iphigenia's conflation with Artemis.
14. See Arnott 1973 and Taplin 1977: 11 with n.3 for other examples of surprise entries in Euripides.

15 Cropp 2000: 178 makes these observations on the passage.
16 On the details and intricacies of metrical patterns in this song, see L. Parker 2016: 83–7.
17 On this function of stichomythia in Euripides, and his increased exploitation of the technique in his later plays, see Schwinge 1968 and Seidensticker 1971: 209–20.
18 L. Parker 2016: xcii, and see further 144–6 on the metrical patterns of the choral song at 392–455.
19 On the likelihood of Iphigenia remaining on stage for this choral ode, see L. Parker 2016: 144 on 391 with further references.
20 See Taplin 1977: 73 for further examples of anapaestic announcements accompanying processional or ceremonial entries.
21 On the two sets of attendants in this sequence, see Bain 1981: 37.
22 For more information on Greek writing tablets from the fifth century BCE, see Pöhlmann and West 2012: 3–5.
23 See Mueller 2016: 170–8 for a persuasive analysis of Phaedra's letter as curse tablet.
24 For further discussion of writing as a metaphor for plot in Euripides, see Torrance 2013: 146–57. Mueller 2016: 182 sees Iphigenia's letter as 'a sort of miniaturized version of the play', and observes (183) that 'the letter's material presence on stage directs the viewer's focus to the normally overlooked technologies of communication that enable drama'.
25 On writing as a motif in Greek tragedy, see Torrance 2013: 135–82.
26 For a detailed discussion of how Euripides engages with the Aeschylean recognition scene in *Electra*, see Torrance 2013: 14–33, with further references.
27 Messengers in Greek tragedy often stress that they are witnesses to the events they report. See De Jong 1991: 11 and Barrett 2002: 31–2, 76–7, 195–7, 209–11.
28 On the oddity of storing the spear in the maidens' quarters, see Kyriakou 2006: 274–6. Sansone 1975, followed by O'Brien 1988: 113, sees parallels between Iphigenia and Pelops as figures who are saved by the gods after their fathers have attempted to murder them.

29 For discussion of the variant versions of Pelops's treachery, see O'Brien 1988: 103–6 and Gantz 1993: 540–5.
30 L. Parker 2016: 227–30 gives an expert overview of the typical features of the reunion duet, and of the metres used in this scene between Iphigenia and Orestes.
31 On the crucial importance of Pylades' extraordinary interjection in Aeschylus's *Libation Bearers*, see Marshall 2017: 116–23.
32 Kaimio 1988: 56 believes that Iphigenia's supplication must be figurative rather than physical, and Naiden 2006: 131 is non-committal regarding whether or not references to clasping knees in Euripidean supplication scenes should be taken literally. On the importance of internal 'stage directions' in Greek tragedy, however, see Taplin 1978: 16–19. On Greek supplication, see especially Naiden 2006, who argues, against the position of Gould 1973, that the person supplicated was not ritually obliged to accept the request.
33 For further examples of Euripidean characters falling to the ground, see Mossman 1999: 57–8 and n.37.
34 For discussion of the metrical details of 1089–152, see L. Parker 2016: 280–2.
35 On the identification of this figure as Artemis, see Hall 2013: 83.
36 For more information about these Athenian religious festivals, see R. Parker 2005: 253–69, 478, and on the significance of the Plynteria for the deceptive ritual in *Iphigenia among the Taurians*, see Sourvinou-Inwood 2003: 302–3 and McClure 2017: 119.
37 On the cleansing of blood pollution with the blood of young sacrificial animals, see R. Parker 1983: 370–4.
38 On the relationship between dithyramb and tragedy, see Battezzato 2013.
39 For this type of messenger speech in Euripides, see De Jong 1991: 18.
40 The text at 1469–70 is unreasonably abrupt and most editors of the text posit that several lines are missing; see Cropp 2000: 264.
41 Mastronarde 1990: 283 and Cropp 2000: 260–1 favour the appearance on a crane, while Hourmouziades 1965: 167 and L. Parker 2016: 342–3 argue against its use.
42 Torrance 2013: 43–6.

43 Halliwell 1986: 181–3, Hall 2013: 69–72.
44 Hunter 1985: 116–17 and 24–35. See also Porter 2000 on the pervasive influence of Euripides in Menandrian comedy.
45 Hall 2013.
46 The transmitted ending of Euripides' *Iphigenia at Aulis*, in which Iphigenia is saved, was probably not part of the original play. See Michelakis 2006: 110–14.
47 See Kitto 1961: 311–29, Conacher 1967: 303–13, Burnett 1971: 71–2, Caldwell 1975: 34, Knox 1979: 250–74, Sutton 1980: 184–90, Seidensticker 1982: 199–211, and Segal 1995; cf. Cropp 2000: 42.
48 L. Parker 2016: xxx, and Amiech and Amiech 2017 xxvii, respectively.
49 Belfiore 1992: 360.
50 Sansone 1975, and Wright 2005.
51 Gregory 2000, Mastronarde 2000 and 2010: 44–62.

2 Characters and Chorus

1 For further discussion of the conventions of Greek tragic performance, see Easterling 1997.
2 See Hall 2002 and 2006: 288–320 on the vocal skills on ancient Greek actors.
3 The point is made by Hall 2006: 316.
4 On the conflation of marriage and death in *Iphigenia at Aulis*, see Foley 1985: 65–105.
5 Tzanetou 2000: 202.
6 On Euripides' plays of voluntary self-sacrifice, see Wilkins 1990.
7 This point is made also by Saïd 2002b: 48.
8 The sources for the Europa myth are discussed by Gantz 1993: 210.
9 Foley 1993: 34.
10 Hartigan 1991: 95–6. Lange 2002: 102–15 follows a different but related track arguing that *Iphigenia among the Taurians* shares narrative features with the *nostos* (i.e. 'homecoming') motif of the *Odyssey*.
11 References for Iphigenia's association with Hecate are given by Ekroth 2003: 72–3 n.67.

12 On the Clashing Rocks representing passage to the Underworld, see Nelis 2001: 234 with n.35. Jason and the Argonauts also pass through the Clashing Rocks, as reported in Euripides' *Medea* (2).
13 On the divine causes of Greek tragic madness, see further Padel 1995: 3–10.
14 The simile occurs frequently in the *Iliad*, but is also used of Odysseus in the *Odyssey*. See Coffey 1957: 118 and Moulton 1977: 139.
15 See Cropp 2000: 195 on these points.
16 On the theme of social status in Euripides' *Electra*, see Roisman 2017: 176–7 with further references.
17 Orestes foams from his mouth and eyes in *Orestes* (220), foam drips into the beard of the mad Heracles (*Her.* 934), and the mouth of Agave, who is possessed, drips foam as she gets ready to kill her son in *Bacchae* (1122).
18 For further contextualization of Aristotle's view within Greek ethics of friendship, see M.W. Blundell 1989: 35–7.
19 On the Greek ideals of friendship, see the observations of Gill 1996: 329–30.
20 Examples include the title characters of Sophocles' *Ajax* (79, 303, 367) and *Antigone* (839), as well as Creon in the latter play (483, 647), Electra and Orestes in Sophocles' *Electra* (807, 1153, 1295, cf. 277), and Medea in Euripides' *Medea* (383, 404, 797, 1049–50, 1355, 1362).
21 This is not always the case in the reception history of *Iphigenia among the Taurians*, where Thoas can be made to desire Iphigenia romantically. See Chapter 5.
22 Hommel 1980: 36 perhaps goes too far in suggesting that Thoas is a doublet of Achilles in Euripides' play, though he makes the interesting point (35) that Iphigenia ends up on Leuke as Achilles' bride after death in some versions of the myth.
23 For further discussion of the theme of persuasion in Greek tragedy, see Buxton 1982.
24 L. Parker 2016: 292, with further judicious comments.
25 De Jong 1991 shows that messengers in Euripides are not mere functionaries, and that 'no narrative is ever objective' (65). Barrett 2002 also stresses the dissociability of speech from the speaker in his study of

the wide variety of figures that can be cast as messengers in Greek tragedy.
26 On Taurian pastoralism, see further Chapter 3.
27 See Wright 2005: 212–13 on the significance of the sea in this 'improbable scenario' (212), and Hall 2013: 47–8 on the importance of the maritime location more generally.
28 Hose 1998: 52–3, for example, argues that Aristotle's condemnation of the Euripidean Chorus is not as categorical as it first appears, making a proposition similar to that of Padel 1974: 240 n.5. Detailed analyses of specific Choruses in Euripides' *Hecuba* and *Andromache* by Mossman 1999: 69–93 and by Allan 2000: 196–232, respectively, have demonstrated their importance. For a general overview of the connection and relevance of Euripidean choral odes, see Mastronarde 2010: 126–52. Nevertheless, the charge of irrelevance is repeated in some scholarship. Sommerstein 2002: 57, for example, suggests that in 'plays such as *Helen* and *Iphigeneia in Tauris*, the chorus have little function'.
29 Swift 2010: 173–240, esp. 197–218.
30 On the identity and function of the Chorus in Euripides' *Helen*, see Burian 2007: 16–23.
31 The halcyon was identified with the kingfisher, but was also a literary creation whose cry was associated by the Greeks with the sound of human lamentation. See L. Parker 2016: 283 with further references.
32 My translation here is meant to reflect the emphasis on the pronouns due to their position in the Greek line. A more literal idiomatic translation into English loses the emphasis on the pronouns: 'An Argive ship will lead *you* home, mistress' . . . 'but you will leave *me* behind here . . .'.
33 On interpreting the text, see L. Parker 2016: 96–100. The quarrel is related in more detail in Euripides' *Electra* (699–746) and *Orestes* (996–1012).
34 For further discussion of the thematic significance of dreams in *Iphigenia among the Taurians*, see Trieschnigg 2008.
35 See Cropp 2000: 247–9 for an overview of mythological sources on Apollo's takeover of the Delphic oracle.

36 Furley 1995: 38.
37 Mastronarde 2010: 142.
38 Wright 2005: 278–97 gives a detailed analysis of the interaction of reality, illusion, and delusion in *Iphigenia among the Taurians*, as well as in *Helen* and the fragments of *Andromeda*.
39 Hall 2013: 233–4.

3 Ethnicity and Gender

1 On the theme of freedom vs. slavery in Aeschylus's *Persians*, see Hall 1989: 97–8 and 1996: 13, 21–2, 112, Harrison 2000a: 76–91, and Rosenbloom 2006: 54–5.
2 In his discussion of different religious practices, for example, Herodotus assumes that all people worship the same gods, identifying the Egyptian Ammon and the Babylonian Baal-Marduk as the Greek Zeus, for instance (Hdt. 1.181, 2.42, 3.158). On this tendency in Herodotus and other Greek authors, see Rudhardt 2002. That is not to say that Herodotus does not notice differences in the religious practices of Greeks and non-Greeks (see Harrison 2000b: 208–22). On the subversion of national stereotypes in Herodotus more generally, see Pelling 1997.
3 Saïd 2002a: 99 refers us to the sophists Hippias (whose views are reported in Plato's *Protagoras* 337c), and a fragment of Antiphon (now [37] ANTIPH. D38b in Laks and Most 2016). Saïd 2002a is an English translation of the original 1984 article.
4 For a full survey and analysis, see Saïd 2002a and Hall 1989: 211–23.
5 On *Medea*'s masculine characteristics, see Foley 2001: 243–71. Foley's arguments have been influential among scholars, though it should be noticed that Mossman 2011: 31–9 disagrees with Foley's analysis. On Theseus's song, see Hall 2006: 314–15.
6 For archaeological information on Taurian settlements, see the comments of Asheri, Lloyd and Corcella 2007: 654, with further references.
7 The stoning of Orestes (and Electra) is referred to at *Orestes* 50, 442, 536, 564, 614, 625, 863, 914; cf. 1477.

8   For further information on the Athenian practice of stoning, see Rosivach 1987.
9   Papadopoulou 2005a: 137–51 gives an illuminating assessment of the motif of the bow in Euripides' *Heracles* and within the broader cultural context of classical Greece.
10 The argument is made by Hall 1989: 122, and cf. West 1992: 121 who states that conch shells are attributed to 'some foreign peoples not civilized enough to have war trumpets'.
11 This point is made by West 1992: 122, with n.193, and see West 1992: 119 for trumpets used on the battlefield.
12 Amiech and Amiech 2017: 63 also suggest that the Taurian herdsmen are not really different from Greek ones, aside from their intention to deliver the Greeks to be sacrificed. Saïd 2002b draws interesting parallels between the Taurians and the Greeks, but goes too far in suggesting (53) that the Taurians have not yet engaged in the practice of human sacrifice.
13 The poetic word *koiranos* 'king' refers to Agamemnon in Aeschylus (*Ag.* 549), to Theseus in Sophocles (*OC* 1287), and to Creon, king of Corinth in Euripides (*Med.* 71).
14 McClure 2017: 117.
15 On foreign music, allusions to foreign music, and male song used to characterize foreigners in Greek tragedy, see Hall 1989: 129–32 and 2006: 315–18.
16 In Sophocles' *Oedipus the King* (387), Oedipus rejects the prophet Tiresias, calling him a *magos*, and in Euripides' *Orestes* (1498) the Phrygian slave reports Helen's inexplicable disappearance as possibly effected by the crafts of sorcerers (*magoi*). On the negative connotations of the *magos* in classical Greece, see Hall 1989: 194 n.107 and Graf 1997: 21.
17 Hesk 2000 shows that deception is not always associated with negative morality in Athenian culture.
18 On the role of Iphigenia as a creator of fictions and its connection with the motifs of writing and weaving, see Torrance 2013: 152–7.
19 Zeitlin 2011: 452 argues that Iphigenia's deception 'carries with it an important truth: Orestes, as a matricide, did pollute the goddess and her sanctuary'.

20 L. Parker 2016: 292 emphasizes that Thoas 'asks shrewd and pertinent questions' in this scene.
21 See Chapter 2 on the repeated allusions to Iphigenia's sacrifice.
22 Laks and Most 2016: [31] PROT. D9, cf. Plato *Theaetetus* 166d–167d.
23 Laks and Most 2016: [27] ATOM. D202, cf. Diels and Kranz 1922: 82 B11a30 = Laks and Most 2016: [32] GORG. D25.
24 Laks and Most 2016: [26] ARCH. D22. Dillon 2004: 64–7 identifies the three different Euripidean approaches to the *nomos-physis* debate mentioned here. For further discussion of the *nomos-physis* theme in Euripides, see Conacher 1998: 84–107.
25 McClure 1999: 170–83, Allan 2000: 121–36.
26 Thomas 2000: 102–34 shows that considerations of ethnic customs (*nomoi*) are the dominant element in Herodotus's ethnographic approach rather than a Greek-barbarian antithesis.
27 For a detailed analysis of the significance of *xenia* in Greek culture, see Herman 1987.
28 Hall 2013: 135–41 addresses the connection between the cult of Diana of the Wood and Euripides' *Iphigenia among the Taurians* in an illuminating discussion.
29 See Chapter 4 for further assessment of this passage.
30 Orestes and Pylades are referred to as Greeks just three times (247, 459, 495), and are otherwise designated as *xenoi* (246, 248, 250, 278, 281, 304, 315, 336, 337, 342, 344, 468, 479, 509, 547, 579, 612, 728, 1081, 1154, 1168, 1178, 1186, 1188, 1204, 1206, 1217, 1222, 1225, 1300, 1315, 1324, 1329, 1333, 1340, 1353).
31 Asheri, Lloyd and Corcella 2007: 262. For a nuanced discussion of the connections between Greek medical beliefs and Herodotus's 'ethnography of health', see Thomas 2000: 28–74.
32 Bacon 1961, esp. 167–72.
33 On the frustrating lack of evidence for women's presence at the theatre in Athens, see Goldhill 1997: 62–6.
34 The bibliography on women in classical Athens is voluminous. Useful starting points for further information are Pomeroy 1975, Cohen 1989, S. Blundell 1998, and Cox 1998.
35 See Hall 1997: 103–10 for further discussion of this phenomenon.

36 Kron 1996: 141, cited by McClure 2017: 120.
37 Detailed information on these four priesthoods of prominence is gathered and assessed by Connelly 2007: 57–83.
38 Hall 2013: 35 suggests that Iphigenia's role most closely resembles that of the title character in Aristophanes' *Lysistrata*, who is also a priestess thought to be modelled after the historical priestess of Athena Polias named Lysimache. See McClure 2017 for further discussion of Iphigenia as a priestess.
39 Connelly 2007: 92. On the significance of the key, see also Bremmer 2013: 91 and McClure 2017: 119–20.
40 See Connelly 2007: 40–1, 157–61.
41 On the significance of the *genos* 'family' and its history in this play, see Mirto 1995.
42 On the connections between weaving and plotting in *Iphigenia among the Taurians*, see Torrance 2013: 40–1.
43 McClure 2017: 124–5.
44 On many levels, *Iphigenia among the Taurians* is an intertextual response to Aeschylus's *Oresteia*. For further discussion, see Caldwell 1975, Aélion 1983: 145–61, Garner 1990: 170–2, Goff 2004: 338–50, Zeitlin 2005, Torrance 2013: 33–45, and Chapter 4: 90–1, 96 in this volume.
45 See Demosthenes, *Against Boeotus I* (39) 22, and Isaeus, *On the Estate of Pyrrhus* (3) 30.
46 Hall 2013: 56.
47 Sourvinou-Inwood 1991: 231, although Sourvinou-Inwood's suggestion that the 'happy ending' of the choral song foreshadows the 'happy ending' of the play is not wholly convincing.
48 Goff 2004: 349.
49 Hall 2006: 257.
50 See Hall 2006: 257 and 264.
51 On barbarians who cannot swim, see Hall 2006: 269–70.
52 On the broad parallels between the experiences of Iphigenia and Orestes, see Sansone 1975: 283–7, Wolff 1992: 325–8, and Zeitlin 2011: 454–6.
53 The point is made by Goff 2004: 340–1.

4 Ritual and the Gods

1. For a detailed survey and analysis of the significance of religious concerns in Greek tragedy, see Sourvinou-Inwood 2003.
2. On the features of dithyrambic lyric, see Chapter 1: 23–4.
3. On the City Dionysia and other dramatic festivals, see further Pickard-Cambridge 1988 and Csapo and Slater 1994: 103–38.
4. For an introduction to Greek religion, see Burkert 1985 and R. Parker 2011, and for an in-depth study of Athenian religious practices, see R. Parker 2005.
5. This kind of mimesis seems to have occurred, however, in Euripides' *Suppliant Women*, which features war orphans on stage. See Morwood 2007: 231.
6. Goff 2004: 338–9.
7. Euripides refers to Titans whereas we know that the iconography associated with Athena depicted the battle with the Giants (the Gigantomachy). It has often been assumed that Euripides simply conflated Titans and Giants, but Stamatopoulou 2012 argues that the mistake is deliberately designed to emphasize Iphigenia's distance and isolation from Greece, and connects her with the Trojan women of Euripides' earlier *Hecuba*, where a similar reference appears.
8. Scullion 2000 argues that cult aetiologies in tragedy are largely invented; Seaford 2009 argues, by contrast, that these aetiologies are significant in relation to the lived experiences of the audience.
9. For arguments against the importance of religion in the development of tragedy, see esp. Scullion 2002 and 2005, and cf. Rozik 2002. Sourvinou-Inwood 2003, on the other hand, sees religion as central to the experience of tragedy.
10. E.g. Yunis 1988, Mikalson 1991, and Sourvinou-Inwood 2003, esp. 291–458, 469–82.
11. Wildberg 2000 and 2002, and Mastronarde 2010: 156.
12. On the influence of Nietzsche and the Schlegel brothers, see Silk and Stern 1981: 90–380, Behler 1986, and Henrichs 1986.
13. Stinton 1976 was one of the first to argue along these lines. More recently, Wright 2005: 387 concludes that Euripides' escape tragedies represent 'a

fully worked-out, horribly bleak view of the world'. For Mastronarde 2010: 205, the gods in Euripides are 'in most respects traditional'. Lefkowitz 2015, developing a position first put forward in Lefkowitz 1989, argues that Euripides emphasizes the arbitrary and brutal nature of the gods.

14 Hughes 1991: 189. See also O'Connor-Visser 1987, Wilkins 1990, and Bonnechere 1994: 260–72 (though Bonnechere is mistaken to claim (261) that *all* Euripidean victims go willingly to their deaths).
15 On the significance of metaphors from animal sacrifice for understanding Euripidean drama, see Foley 1985: 30–64 and Henrichs 2000.
16 Bremmer 2013, with 90–1 on conducting sacrifices with a sword, and 94–5 on the holocaust.
17 Reasons for doubting the account of Themistocles' human sacrifices are discussed by Hughes 1991: 112–15.
18 Henrichs 1981: 232, and Hughes 1991: 185.
19 Novichenkova 1996: 202. O'Bryhim 2000 suggested that Euripides was inspired by ancient Phoenician practices of human sacrifice but the argument has not generated much traction, and there are significant differences in spite of some similarities. The bones of victims unearthed at Carthage and Sousse, for example, 'belonged to infants and young children' (O'Bryhim 2000: 32), whereas the Taurians seems to sacrifice only adult male victims from outside their own community.
20 Evidence on the conflation of Iphigenia with Artemis is gathered by Lyons 1997: 134–72.
21 On the parallels between Iphigenia and Artemis in the play, see also Wolff 1992: 320, Zeitlin 2011: 452, and McClure 2017: 121–2.
22 These different terms for statues are discussed by Burkert 1985: 89–92, 187, Steiner 2001: 102 with n.95, and Bremmer 2013: 95.
23 McClure 2017: 121.
24 The more common word for temple, *naos*, also used throughout the play, similarly refers to the dwelling place of the god (Burkert 1985: 88). On the association of female ritual activity with domestic duties, see Goff 2004: 51–69.
25 Goff 2004: 345.
26 Cropp 2000: 262 gives a summary of the excavations and analyses of the fifth-century temple in his comments on line 1453. On earlier

religious activity at the site, see McInerney 2015: 291, with further references.
27 On the cults of Artemis Tauropolos in Asia Minor, see Graf 1985: 410–17.
28 For a general overview of Artemis's spheres of influence, see Burkert 1985: 149–52 and Cole 1998. See also Vernant 1998: 11–30 on Artemis's otherness and liminality, and Marinatos 2000 on her evolution from 'mistress of animals' to patron of warriors.
29 For other examples of etymological games in Euripides, see Torrance 2013: 97–100.
30 These arguments are made by McInerney 2015: 298–303, with further references. Kowalzig 2013 also argues that *Iphigenia among the Taurians* engages with contemporary issues of trade and travel.
31 For further arguments in support of reading the ritual at Halai as a male initiation ritual, see Lloyd-Jones 1983: 96–7.
32 Cropp 2000: 54.
33 On the different versions of the final destination for Artemis's statue, see Graf 1979 and Hall 2013: 135–9.
34 McInerney 2015: 311.
35 Ceccarelli 2004: 99–101.
36 McInerney 2015: 290. Hall 2013: xxx notes that the Athenian theatre audience will have been aware of the sanctuary of Artemis Brauronia in their vicinity as they watched Euripides' play.
37 Sourvinou-Inwood 1988 is the most detailed discussion of the *arkteia*.
38 For further information on this myth and its significance, see Brelich 1969: 248–9, Vernant 1991: 215–16, and Burkert 1992: 75.
39 Tzanetou 2000. For Tzanetou (212–13), it is not only Iphigenia's ritual journey but also that of Orestes which 'may have been *dramatically* conceived according to the paradigm of the female rites in ... Brauron' (emphasis original).
40 Ekroth 2003, with detailed references regarding the various propositions of scholars for identifying worship of Iphigenia at Brauron.
41 On dedications to Artemis at Brauron, see Linders 1972 and Kahil 1983, and for a more general discussion, see Cole 1998: 36–42.
42 Ekroth 2003: 96.
43 Mirto 1995: 95–6.

44 Zeitlin 2011: 465.
45 Lloyd-Jones 1983, esp. 98–101.
46 Ekroth 2003: 99.
47 On sacrilegious crime and its penalties in classical Athens, see Cohen 1991: 203–17.
48 For more detail on the *Anthesteria* festival as a whole, see Burkert 1983: 213–43, Hamilton 1992, Robertson 1993, and R. Parker 2005: 290–316.
49 Davidson 1998: 36–69, esp. 61–9, discusses Athenian drinking practices and the types of cups they used.
50 On the Areopagus as a homicide court and Aeschylus's *Eumenides*, see Sommerstein 1989: 13–17.
51 The uncanny aspects of the *Choes* are discussed by R. Parker 2005: 294–5.
52 For further details and references on the *Choes*, see R. Parker 2005: 297–301, with 210 on ceremonies marking male teenage transitions at Athens.
53 See, e.g. Sourvinou-Inwood 1991: 231, Cropp 2000: 201, and L. Parker 2016: 143.
54 E.g. Goff 1999: 122, Wolff 1992: 329 and n.60, and Mastronarde 2010: 164.
55 Sansone 1975: 288–9 argues persuasively that this is how we should understand Iphigenia's reference to the feast. Cropp 2000: 202 suggests that Iphigenia is saying the feast occurred but Tantalus did not serve Pelops's flesh.
56 Papadopoulou 2005b.
57 Trieschnigg 2008.
58 On this issue, see further Torrance 2013: 34–8.
59 Zeitlin 2011: 466.
60 Hartigan 1991: 103–4 discusses Athena's unexpected appearance.
61 Cropp 2000: 257, and L. Parker 2016: 333.

5 Reception

1 Hall 2013. This chapter is much indebted to Hall's brilliant study. For a briefer but nevertheless valuable overview of the play's reception in literature, the fine arts, and on stage and screen, see Mills 2015. Reid

1993: 605–7 remains an important first point of reference for sources dealing with the Taurian legend.
2. Ingleheart 2010: 223, and *passim* for more detailed argumentation on how Ovid's text is directly influenced by Euripides. On the use of the term *axenos* in *Iphigenia among the Taurians*, see Chapter 1: 6–7.
3. Hall 2013: 102.
4. Ingleheart 2010: 231.
5. See Hall 2013: 105–6.
6. Hall 2013: 120.
7. For further information on this text, see Santelia 1991 and Hall 2013: 117–21.
8. On Rucellai's *Oreste*, see further Di Maria 1996 and Hall 2013: 161–6.
9. See Gliksohn 1985, esp. 228–32, and Heitner 1964 on eighteenth-century dramas.
10. Hall 2013: 178–9.
11. See further Gliksohn 1985: 154–8, 170–1.
12. Matthiessen 2000: 369, and Lee 2003: 70.
13. Cf. Hall 2013: 179.
14. E.g. Heitner 1964: 308, Matthiessen 2000: 370, Torrance 2007, and Hall 2013: 206–30.
15. On Goethe's abilities for reading Greek, see Trevelyan 1981: 24, 96–103.
16. Torrance 2007: 190, and cf. Kerry 2001: 42 on the metaphor of a familial relationship distancing Goethe's Thoas from Iphigenie as a potential suitor.
17. Hall 2013: 208.
18. Hall 2013: 214–15.
19. Hall and Macintosh 2005: 48.
20. Hall 2013: 210 (emphasis original).
21. Hall and Macintosh 2005: 49.
22. Geyer-Ryan 1985, and Hall 2013: 219–24.
23. Hall 2009: 28.
24. Ewans 2008: 233–4 gives an overview of Guillard's adaptation of de la Touche's play. On the 'inspiration-chain', which may have influenced both Gluck and Goethe to work on the Taurian legend at the same time, see Phillippo 2003: 19–21.

25 Gliksohn 1985: 171.
26 See Hall 2013: 198–9, with further references.
27 Goldhill 2010: 224.
28 Ewans 2008: 232, Goldhill 2010: 217, and Hall 2013 186–8.
29 Hall 2013: 191.
30 Hall 2013: 179.
31 Zanobi 2010: 254.
32 Foley 2012: 41–2, Hall 2013: 245–6, and Slater 2015: 167, 171–2. For (black and white) photographs from the production, see Slater 2015.
33 Hall 2013: 251–5, developing the observations of Post 1930.
34 Barrenechea 2015: 259–61.
35 Hall 2013: 277.
36 Pulford 2013: 204. For further discussion of Nowras engagement with *Iphigenia among the Taurians*, see Hall 2013: 287–92.
37 Hall 2013: 93–101.
38 Hall 2013: 100–1, with further references.
39 Ingleheart 2010: 238.
40 As ní Mheallaigh 2014: 39–71 has argued, the dialogue shifts from being a competition on the theme of friendship to 'a contest in (and a commentary on) novelistic narrative'.
41 On the *Erotes* treatise and on Augustine's references to Orestes and Pylades, see Hall 2013: 107–10.
42 Hall 2013: 165.
43 Hall and Macintosh 2005: 45–6.
44 Gliksohn 1985: 175.
45 Heitner 1964: 296.
46 Gliksohn 1985: 218, and Torrance 2007: 180, 184.
47 Becker-Cantarino 2002.
48 Frevert 1989: 19.
49 For further elaboration on Goethe's representation of gender in *Iphigenie auf Tauris*, see Torrance 2007.
50 Hall 2013: 211.
51 Hall 2013: 213.
52 On Winckelmann's influence, see e.g. Pfeiffer 1976 167–73.
53 Boyle 1992: 385.

54 See Hall 2013: 242 for a clear photograph of the costume, and cf. Slater 2015: 169.
55 Foley 2012: 82–3.
56 Zanobi 2010: 241.
57 Zanobi 2010: 242.
58 Foley 2012: 236.
59 Hall 2013: 265.
60 Foley 2012: 235.
61 Hall 2013: 271–2.
62 Hall 2013: 268–9.
63 Hall 2013: 268.
64 Information on Harrison's *Iphigenia in Crimea* has been retrieved from the BBC website. See http://www.bbc.co.uk/programmes/b08n1ylb (accessed 13 September 2018).
65 Peter Meineck and Bryan Doerries have both brought Greek tragedy to US war veterans and to mainstream audiences. Meineck is the founder and program director of Aquila Theatre, which reinterprets classical plays for a contemporary audience, with particular attention to war veterans, and program director of The Warrior Chorus, which trains veterans to deliver veteran and scholar-led public programming across a broad range of cultural centres in the US. Doerries is artistic director of Theater of War productions, founded in 2009, that uses Greek tragedy to address issues of trauma related to veteran communities.
66 Hall 2013: 151–3, drawing on Bielfeldt 2005: 167–332.
67 For a detailed survey, with illuminating analysis, see Hall 2013: 158–82.
68 Hall 2013: 161.
69 See further Hall and Macintosh 2005: 44–54.
70 Cf. Gliksohn 1985: 209.
71 Cf. Gliksohn 1985: 205.
72 Nisbet 2002: 219.
73 On the Christian imagery of the play, see Torrance 2007 for further details.
74 See further Hall 2013: 281–4.
75 Hall 2013: 292, and see also 177–82 on Catherine the Great's admiration for the play and its connections with her foreign policies in the Black

Sea. L. Parker 2016: 303, and xvi n.4 also notes some parallels between the statue of Artemis and 'Black Virgins'.

76 Foley 2012: 236–7 makes this remark regarding recent adaptations of *Iphigenia among the Taurians* in the US, but the insightful assessment could also be applied to most, if not all, of the works discussed in this chapter.

Bibliography

Aélion, R. (1983), *Euripide Héritier d'Eschyle, Volume I*, Paris: Les Belles Lettres.
Allan, W. (2000), *The Andromache and Euripidean Tragedy*, Oxford: Oxford University Press.
Amiech, C. and L. Amiech (eds) (2017), *Euripide: Iphigénie en Tauride*, Paris: Les Belles Lettres.
Arnott, G. (1973), 'Euripides and the Unexpected', *Greece & Rome* 20: 49–64.
Asheri, D., A. Lloyd and A. Corcella (eds) (2007), *A Commentary on Herodotus Books I–IV*, Oxford: Oxford University Press.
Bacon, H. (1961), *Barbarians in Greek Tragedy*, New Haven, CT: Yale University Press.
Bain, D. (1981), *Masters, Servants and Orders in Greek Tragedy: A Study of Some Aspects of Dramatic Technique and Convention*, Manchester: Manchester University Press.
Barrenechea, F. (2015), 'Greek Tragedy in Mexico', in K. Bosher, F. Macintosh, J. McConnell and P. Rankine (eds), *The Oxford Handbook of Greek Drama in the Americas*, Oxford: Oxford University Press, 252–70.
Barrett, J. (2002), *Staged Narrative: Poetics and the Messenger in Greek Tragedy*, Berkeley, CA: University of California Press.
Battezzato, L. (2013), 'Dithyramb and Greek Tragedy', in B. Kowalzig and P. Wilson (eds), *Dithyramb in Context*, Oxford: Oxford University Press, 93–110.
Becker-Cantarino, B. (2002), 'Goethe and Gender', in L. Sharpe (ed.), *The Cambridge Companion to Goethe*, Cambridge: Cambridge University Press, 179–92.
Behler, E. (1986), 'A.W. Schlegel and the Nineteenth-Century *damnatio* of Euripides', *Greek, Roman and Byzantine Studies* 27: 335–67.
Belfiore, E. (1992), 'Aristotle and Iphigenia', in A. Rorty (ed.), *Essays on Aristotle's Poetics*, Princeton, NJ: Princeton University Press, 359–77.
Bielfeldt, R. (2005), *Orestes auf römischen Sarkophagen*, Berlin: Reimer Verlag.

Blundell, M.W. (1989), *Helping Friends and Harming Enemies: A Study in Sophocles and Greek Ethics*, Cambridge: Cambridge University Press.

Blundell, S. (1998), *Women in Classical Athens*, London: Bristol Classical Press.

Bonnechere, P. (1994), *Le Sacrifice Humain en Grèce Ancienne*, Athens and Liège: Centre International d'Étude de la Religion Grecque Antique.

Boyle, N. (1992), *Goethe the Poet and the Age Volume I: The Poetry of Desire 1749–1790*, Oxford: Oxford University Press.

Braund, D. (1994), *Georgia in Antiquity: A History of Colchis and Transcaucasian Iberia 550 BC–AD 562*, Oxford: Oxford University Press.

Brelich, A. (1969), *Paides e Parthenoi*, Rome: Edizioni dell' Ateneo.

Bremmer, J. (2013), 'Human Sacrifice in Euripides' *Iphigenia in Tauris*: Greek and Barbarian', in P. Bonnechere and R. Gagné (eds), *Sacrifices Humains: Perspectives Croisées et Représentations*, Liège: Liège University Press, 87–100.

Burian, P. (ed.) (2007), *Euripides: Helen*, Oxford: Aris & Phillips.

Burkert, W. (1983), *Homo Necans: The Anthropology of Ancient Greek Sacrificial Ritual and Myth*, trans. P. Bing, Berkeley, CA: University of California Press.

Burkert, W. (1985), *Greek Religion*, trans. J. Raffan, Cambridge, MA: Harvard University Press.

Burkert, W. (1992), *The Orientalizing Revolution: Near Eastern Influence on Greek Culture in the Early Archaic Age*, trans. M.E. Pinder, Cambridge, MA: Harvard University Press.

Burnett, A.P. (1971), *Catastrophe Survived: Euripides' Plays of Mixed Reversal*, Oxford: Clarendon Press.

Buxton, R. (1982), *Persuasion in Greek Tragedy*, Cambridge: Cambridge University Press.

Caldwell, R. (1975), 'Tragedy Romanticized: The *Iphigenia Taurica*', *Classical Journal* 70: 23–40.

Carson, A. (2014), *Euripides: Iphigenia among the Taurians*, Chicago, IL: University of Chicago Press.

Ceccarelli, P. (2004), 'Dancing the *Pyrrhichē* in Athens', in P. Murray and P. Wilson (eds), *Music and the Muses: The Culture of Mousikē in the Classical Athenian City*, Oxford: Oxford University Press, 91–118.

Coffey, M. (1957), 'The Function of the Homeric Simile', *American Journal of Philology* 78: 113–32.

Cohen, D. (1989), 'Seclusion, Separation, and the Status of Women in Classical Athens', *Greece & Rome* 36: 3–15.

Cohen, D. (1991), *Law, Sexuality, and Society: The Enforcement of Morals in Classical Athens*, Cambridge: Cambridge University Press.

Cole, S. (1998), 'Domesticating Artemis', in S. Blundell and M. Williamson (eds), *The Sacred and the Feminine in Ancient Greece*, London: Routledge, 27–43.

Conacher, D.J. (1967), *Euripidean Drama: Myth, Theme, and Structure*, Toronto: University of Toronto Press.

Conacher, D.J. (1998), *Euripides and the Sophists*, London: Duckworth.

Connelly, J.B. (2007), *Portrait of a Priestess: Women and Ritual in Ancient Greece*, Princeton, NJ: Princeton University Press.

Cox, C. (1998), *Household Interests: Property, Marriage Strategies, and Family Dynamics in Ancient Athens*, Princeton, NJ: Princeton University Press.

Cropp, M. (ed.) (2000), *Euripides: Iphigenia in Tauris*, Warminster: Aris & Phillips.

Csapo, E. and W.J. Slater (1994), *The Context of Ancient Drama*, Ann Arbor, MI: The University of Michigan Press.

D'Angour, A. (2009), 'Language and Meter', *Language & History* 52: 59–69.

Davidson, J. (1998), *Courtesans and Fishcakes: The Consuming Passions of Classical Athens*, New York: St Martin's Press.

De Jong, I. (1991), *Narrative in Drama: The Art of the Euripidean Messenger Speech*, Leiden: Brill.

Diels, H. and W. Kranz (1922), *Die Fragmente der Vorsokratiker* (3 vols) Berlin: Weidmann.

Diggle, J. (1981), *Euripidis Fabulae Tomus II: Supplices, Electra, Hercules, Troades, Iphigenia in Tauris, Ion*, Oxford: Oxford University Press.

Dillon, J. (2004), 'Euripides and the Philosophy of His Time', *Classics Ireland* 11: 47–73.

Di Maria, S. (1996), 'Towards an Italian Theater: Rucellai's Oreste', *Modern Languages Notes* 111(1): 123–48.

Easterling, P. (1997), 'Form and Performance', in P. Easterling (ed.), *The Cambridge Companion to Greek Tragedy*, Cambridge: Cambridge University Press, 151–77.

Ekroth, G. (2003), 'Inventing Iphigeneia? On Euripides and the Cultic Construction of Brauron', *Kernos* 16: 59–118.

Ewans, M. (2008), '*Iphigénie en Tauride* and *Elektra*: "Apolline" and "Dionysiac" Receptions of Greek Tragedy into Opera', in L. Hardwick and C. Stray (eds), *A Companion to Classical Receptions*, Oxford: Blackwell Publishing, 231–46.

Foley, H. (1985), *Ritual Irony: Poetry and Sacrifice in Euripides*, Ithaca, NY: Cornell University Press.

Foley, H. (1993), *The Homeric Hymn to Demeter: Translation, Commentary, and Interpretive Essays*, Princeton, NJ: Princeton University Press.

Foley, H. (2001), *Female Acts in Greek Tragedy*, Princeton, NJ: Princeton University Press.

Foley, H. (2012), *Reimagining Greek Tragedy on the American Stage*, Princeton, NJ: Princeton University Press.

Frevert, U. (1989), *Women in German History: From Bourgeois Emancipation to Sexual Liberation*, trans. S. McKinnon, New York: St Martin's Press.

Furley, W. (1995), 'Praise and Persuasion in Greek Hymns', *Journal of Hellenic Studies* 115: 29–46.

Gantz, T. (1993), *Early Greek Myth: A Guide to Literary and Artistic Sources*, Baltimore, MD: Johns Hopkins University Press.

Garland, R. (1990), 'Priests and Power in Classical Athens', in M. Beard and J. North, *Pagan Priests: Religion and Power in the Ancient World*, New York: Cornell University Press, 73–91.

Garner, R. (1990), *From Homer to Tragedy: The Art of Allusion in Greek Poetry*, London: Routledge.

Geyer-Ryan, H. (1985), 'Prefigurative Racism in Goethe's *Iphigenie auf Tauris*', in F. Barker, P. Hulme, M. Iversen and D. Loxley (eds), *Europe and its Others: Proceedings of the Essex Conference on the Sociology of Literature*, Vol. I, Colchester: University of Essex Press, 112–19.

Gill, C. (1996), *Personality in Greek Epic, Tragedy, and Philosophy*, Oxford: Oxford University Press.

Gliksohn, J.-M. (1985), *Iphigénie de la Grèce Antique à l'Europe des Lumières*, Paris: Presses Universitaires de France.

Goff, B. (1999), 'The Violence of Community: Ritual in the *Iphigenia in Tauris*', *Bucknell Review* 43: 109–25.

Goff, B. (2004), *Citizen Bacchae: Women's Ritual Practice in Ancient Greece*, Berkeley, CA: University of California Press.
Goff, B. (2009), *Euripides: Trojan Women*, London: Duckworth.
Goldhill, S. (1997), 'The Audience of Athenian Tragedy', in P. Easterling (ed.), *The Cambridge Companion to Greek Tragedy*, Cambridge: Cambridge University Press, 54–68.
Goldhill, S. (2010), 'Who Killed Gluck?', in P. Brown and S. Ograjenšek (eds), *Ancient Drama in Music for the Modern Stage*, Oxford: Oxford University Press, 210–39.
Gould, J. (1973), 'HIKETEIA', *Journal of Hellenic Studies* 93: 74–103.
Graf, F. (1979), 'Das Götterbild aus dem Taurerland', *Antike Welt* 10(4): 33–41.
Graf, F. (1985), *Nordionische Kulte: Religionsgeschichtliche und epigraphische Unterzuchungen zu der Kulten von Chios, Erythrai, Klazomenai und Phokaia*, Rome: Swiss Institute in Rome.
Graf, F. (1997), *Magic in the Ancient World*, trans. F. Philip, Cambridge, MA: Harvard University Press.
Gregory, J. (2000), 'Comic Elements in Euripides', *Illinois Classical Studies* 24–25: 59–74.
Hall, E. (1987), 'The Geography of Euripides' *Iphigeneia among the Taurians*', *American Journal of Philology* 108: 427–33.
Hall, E. (1989), *Inventing the Barbarian: Greek Self-Definition through Tragedy*, Oxford: Oxford University Press.
Hall, E. (ed.) (1996), *Aeschylus: Persians*, Warminster: Aris & Phillips.
Hall, E. (1997), 'The Sociology of Athenian Tragedy', in P. Easterling (ed.), *The Cambridge Companion to Greek Tragedy*, 93–126, Cambridge: Cambridge University Press.
Hall, E. (2002), 'The Singing Actors of Antiquity', in P. Easterling and E. Hall (eds), *Greek and Roman Actors: Aspects of an Ancient Profession*, Cambridge: Cambridge University Press, 3–38.
Hall, E. (2006), *The Theatrical Cast of Athens: Interactions between Ancient Greek Drama and Society*, Oxford: Oxford University Press.
Hall, E. (2009), 'Greek Tragedy and the Politics of Subjectivity in Recent Fiction', *Classical Receptions Journal* 1: 1–17.
Hall, E. (2013), *Adventures with Iphigenia in Tauris: A Cultural History of Euripides' Black Sea Tragedy*, Oxford: Oxford University Press.

Hall, E. and F. Macintosh (2005), *Greek Tragedy and the British Theatre 1660–1914*, Oxford: Oxford University Press.

Halliwell, S. (1986), *Aristotle's Poetics*, London: Duckworth.

Hamilton, R. (1992), *Choes and Anthesteria: Athenian Iconography and Ritual*, Ann Arbor, MI: University of Michigan Press.

Harrison, T. (2000a), *The Emptiness of Asia: Aeschylus' Persians and the History of the Fifth Century*, London: Duckworth.

Harrison, T. (2000b), *Divinity and History: The Religion of Herodotus*, Oxford: Oxford University Press.

Hartigan, K. (1991), *Ambiguity and Self-Deception: The Apollo and Artemis Plays of Euripides*, Frankfurt-am-Main: Peter Lang.

Heitner, R.R. (1964), 'The *Iphigenia in Tauris* Theme in Drama of the Eighteenth Century', *Comparative Literature* 16(4): 289–309.

Henrichs, A. (1981), 'Human Sacrifice in Greek Religion: Three Case Studies', in J. Rudhardt and O. Reverdin (eds), *Le Sacrifice dans l'Antiquité*, Geneva: Fondation Hardt, 195–242.

Henrichs, A. (1986), 'The Last of the Detractors: Friedrich Nietzsche's Condemnation of Euripides', *Greek Roman and Byzantine Studies* 27: 369–97.

Henrichs, A. (2000), 'Drama and *Dromena*: Bloodshed, Violence, and Sacrificial Metaphor in Euripides', *Harvard Studies in Classical Philology* 100: 173–88.

Herman, G. (1987), *Ritualized Friendship and the Greek City*, Cambridge: Cambridge University Press.

Hesk, J. (2000), *Deception and Democracy in Classical Athens*, Cambridge: Cambridge University Press.

Hommel, H. (1980), *Der Gott Achilleus*, Heidelberg: Winter.

Hose, M. (1998), 'Tanz, Gesang – und Partizipation: Über den Chor', in B. Zimmermann (ed.), *Euripides: Iphigenie bei den Taurern*, Stuttgart: M. & P. Verlag für Wissenschaft und Forschung, 51–66.

Hourmouziades, N. (1965), *Production and Imagination in Euripides: Form and Function of the Scenic Space*, Athens: Greek Society for Humanistic Studies.

Hughes, D. (1991), *Human Sacrifice in Ancient Greece*, London: Routledge.

Hunter, R. (1985), *The New Comedy of Greece and Rome*, Cambridge: Cambridge University Press.

Ingleheart, J. (2010), '"I'm a Celebrity, Get Me Out of Here": The Reception of Euripides' *Iphigenia among the Taurians* in Ovid's Exile Poetry', in I. Gildenhard and M. Revermann (eds), *Beyond the Fifth Century: Interactions with Greek Tragedy from the Fourth Century BCE to the Middle Ages*, Leiden: Brill, 219–46.

Kahil, L. (1983), 'Mythological Repertoire of Brauron', in W. Moon (ed.), *Ancient Greek Art and Iconography*, Madison, WI: University of Wisconsin Press, 231–44.

Kaimio, M. (1988), *Physical Contact in Greek Tragedy: A Study of Stage Conventions*, Helsinki: Suomalainen Tiedeakatemia.

Kerry, P.E. (2001), *Enlightenment Thought in the Writings of Goethe*, New York: Camden House.

Kitto, H.D.F. (1961), *Greek Tragedy: A Literary Study*, London: Routledge.

Knox, B. (1979), *Word and Action: Essays on the Ancient Theater*, Baltimore, MD: Johns Hopkins University Press.

Kovacs, D. (ed.) (1999), *Euripides: Trojan Women, Iphigenia among the Taurians, Ion*, Cambridge, MA: Harvard University Press.

Kowalzig, B. (2013), 'Transcultural Chorality: *Iphigeneia in Tauris* and Athenian Imperial Economics in a Polytheistic World', in R. Gagné and M. Hopman (eds), *Choral Meditations in Greek Tragedy*, Cambridge: Cambridge University Press, 178–210.

Kron, U. (1996), 'Priesthoods, Dedications, and Euergetism: What Part Did Religion Play in the Political and Social Status of Greek Women?', in P. Hellström and B. Alroth (eds), *Religion and Power in the Ancient Greek World*, Uppsala: Acta Universitatis Upsaliensis, 139–82.

Kyriakou, P. (2006), *A Commentary on Euripides' Iphigenia in Tauris*, Berlin: De Gruyter.

Laks, A. and G. Most (eds) (2016), *Early Greek Philosophy* (9 vols), Cambridge, MA: Harvard University Press.

Lange, K. (2002), *Euripides und Homer: Untersuchungen zur Homernachwirkung in Elektra, IT, Helena, Orestes und Kyklops*, Stuttgart: Franz Steiner Verlag.

Lee, K. (2003), 'Goethe's *Iphigenie* and Euripides' *Iphigenia in Tauris*', *Journal of the Australasian Universities Language and Literature Association*, Feb.: 64–74.

Lefkowitz, M. (1989), 'Impiety and Atheism in Euripides' Dramas', *Classical Quarterly* 39: 70–82.
Lefkowitz, M. (2015), *Euripides and the Gods*, Oxford: Oxford University Press.
Linders, T. (1972), *Studies in the Treasure Records of Artemis Brauronia*, Stockholm: Swedish Institute in Athens.
Lloyd-Jones, H. (1983), 'Artemis and Iphigenia', *Journal of Hellenic Studies* 103: 87–102.
Lyons, D. (1997), *Gender and Immortality: Heroines in Ancient Greek Myth and Cult*, Princeton, NJ: Princeton University Press.
McClure, L. (1999), *Spoken Like A Woman: Speech and Gender in Athenian Drama*, Princeton, NJ: Princeton University Press.
McClure, L. (2017), 'Priestess and Polis in Euripides' *Iphigeneia in Tauris*', in M. Dillon, E. Eidinow and L. Maurizio (eds), *Women's Ritual Competence in the Greco-Roman Mediterranean*, London: Routledge, 115–30.
McInerney, J. (2015), '"There Will Be Blood...": The Cult of Artemis Tauropolos at Halai Araphenides', in K.F. Daly and L.A. Riccardi (eds), *Cities Called Athens: Studies Honoring John McK. Camp II*, Lewisburg, PA: Bucknell University Press, 289–320.
Marinatos, N. (2000), *The Goddess and the Warrior: The Naked Goddess and the Mistress of Animals in Early Greek Religion*, London: Routledge.
Marshall, C. W. (2017), *Aeschylus: Libation Bearers*, London: Bloomsbury.
Mastronarde, D. (1990), 'Actors on High: The Skene Roof, the Crane, and the Gods in Attic Drama', *Classical Antiquity* 9(2): 247–94.
Mastronarde, D. (2000), 'Euripidean Tragedy and Genre: The Terminology and its Problems', *Illinois Classical Studies*, 24–25: 23–40.
Mastronarde, D. (2010), *The Art of Euripides: Dramatic Technique and Social Context*, Cambridge: Cambridge University Press.
Matthiessen, K. (2000), 'Die Taurische Iphigenie bei Euripides, Geothe, und Anderswo', in S. Gödde and T. Heinze (eds), *Skenika: Beiträge zum antiken Theatre und seiner Rezeption*, Darmstadt: Wissenschaftliche Buchgesellschaft, 363–8.
Michelakis, P. (2006), *Euripides: Iphigenia at Aulis*, London: Duckworth.
Mikalson, J. (1991), *Honor Thy Gods: Popular Religion in Greek Tragedy*, Chapel Hill, NC: University of North Carolina Press.

Mills, S. (2015), 'Iphigenia in Tauris', in R. Lauriola and K.N. Demetriou (eds), *Brill's Companion to the Reception of Euripides*, Leiden: Brill, 259–91.

Mirto, M. (1995), 'Salvare il genos e riformare il culto. Divinazione et razionalità nell' *Ifigenia Taurica*', *Materiali e Discussioni per l'Analisi dei Testi Classici* 32: 55–98.

Morwood, J. (1999), *Euripides' Bacchae and Other Plays: Iphigenia among the Taurians, Bacchae, Iphigenia at Aulis, Rhesus*, Oxford: Oxford University Press.

Morwood, J. (ed.) (2007), *Euripides: Suppliant Women*, Oxford: Aris & Phillips.

Mossman, J. (1999), *Wild Justice: A Study of Euripides' Hecuba*, 2nd edn, London: Bristol Classical Press.

Mossman, J. (ed.) (2011), *Euripides: Medea*, Oxford: Aris & Phillips.

Moulton, C. (1977), *Similes in the Homeric Poems*, Göttingen: Vandenhoeck & Ruprecht.

Mueller, M. (2016), *Objects as Actors: Props and the Poetics of Performance in Greek Tragedy*, Chicago, IL: University of Chicago Press.

Naiden, F. (2006), *Ancient Supplication*, Oxford: Oxford University Press.

Nelis, D. (2001), *Vergil's Aeneid and the Argonautica of Apollonius Rhodius*, Cambridge: Francis Cairns.

ní Mheallaigh, K. (2014), *Reading Fiction with Lucian: Fakes, Freaks and Hyperreality*, Cambridge: Cambridge University Press.

Nisbet, H. B. (2002), 'Religion and Philosophy', in L. Sharpe (ed.), *The Cambridge Companion to Goethe*, Cambridge: Cambridge University Press, 219–31.

Novichenkova, N. G. (1996), 'The Sanctuary of the Crimean Yaila', *Ancient Civilizations from Scythia to Siberia* 3: 181–217.

O'Brien, M. J. (1988), 'Pelopid History and the Plot of *Iphigenia in Tauris*', *Classical Quarterly*, 38: 98–115.

O'Bryhim, S. (2000), 'The Ritual of Human Sacrifice in Euripides, *Iphigenia in Tauris*', *Classical Bulletin* 76: 29–37.

O'Connor-Visser, E.A.M.E. (1987), *Aspects of Human Sacrifice in Euripides*, Amsterdam: B.R. Grüner.

Padel, R. (1974), 'Imagery of the Elsewhere: Two Choral Odes of Euripides', *Classical Quarterly* 24: 227–41.

Padel, R. (1995), *Whom Gods Destroy: Elements of Greek and Tragic Madness*, Princeton, NJ: Princeton University Press.

Papadopoulou, T. (2005a), *Heracles and Euripidean Tragedy*, Cambridge: Cambridge University Press.

Papadopoulou, T. (2005b), 'Artemis and Constructs of Meaning in *Iphigenia in Tauris*', *Ariadne* 11: 107–27.

Parker, L.P.E. (ed.) (2016), *Euripides: Iphigenia in Tauris*, Oxford: Oxford University Press.

Parker, R. (1983), *Miasma: Pollution and Purification in Early Greek Religion*, Oxford: Oxford University Press.

Parker, R. (2005), *Polytheism and Society at Athens*, Oxford: Oxford University Press.

Parker, R. (2011), *On Greek Religion*, Ithaca, NY: Cornell University Press.

Pelling, C. (1997), 'East is East and West is West – Or Are They? National Stereotypes in Herodotus', *Histos* 1: 51–66.

Pfeiffer, R. (1976), *History of Classical Scholarship from 1300 to 1850*, Oxford: Clarendon Press.

Phillippo, S. (2003), '"Inspirationsketten": Inspiration und Innovation im "Nachleben" von Euripides' *Iphigeneia bei den Taurern*', in K. Brodersen (ed.), *Die Antike außerhalb des Hörsaals*, Münster: LIT Verlag, 11–46.

Pickard-Cambridge, A.W. (1988), *The Dramatic Festivals of Athens*, 2nd edn, rev. J. Gould and D.M. Lewis, Oxford: Clarendon Press.

Pöhlmann, E. and M.L. West (2012), 'The Oldest Greek Papyrus and Writing Tablets: Fifth-Century Documents from the "Tomb of the Musician" in Attica', *Zeitschrift für Papyrologie und Epigraphik* 180: 1–16.

Pomeroy, S. (1975), *Goddesses, Whores, Wives, and Slaves: Women in Classical Antiquity*, New York: Schocken Books.

Porter, J. (2000), 'Euripides and Menander: *Epitrepontes*, Act IV', *Illinois Classical Studies* 24–25: 157–73.

Post, L.A. (1930), '*Iphigenia among the Taurians* and *Trader Horn*', *Classical Weekly* 23: 119–20.

Pulford, D. (2013), 'Counter-imperialism in Louis Nowra's *The Golden Age*', *Australian Literary Studies in the 21st Century* Jan.: 204–9.

Race, W. (1997), *Pindar: Nemean Odes, Isthmian Odes, Fragments*, Cambridge, MA: Harvard University Press.

Reid, J.D. (1993), *The Oxford Guide to Classical Mythology in the Arts, 1300–1900s*, Oxford: Oxford University Press.

Robertson, N. (1993), 'Athens' Festival of the New Wine', *Harvard Studies in Classical Philology* 95: 197–250.

Roisman, H. (2017), 'Electra', in L. McClure (ed.), *A Companion to Euripides*, Chichester: John Wiley & Sons, 166–81.

Rosenbloom, D. (2006), *Aeschylus: Persians*, London: Duckworth.

Rosivach, V. (1987), 'Execution by Stoning in Classical Athens', *Classical Antiquity* 6: 232–48.

Rozik, E. (2002), *The Roots of Theatre: Rethinking Ritual and Other Theories of Origin*, Iowa City: Iowa University Press.

Rudhardt, J. (2002), 'The Greek Attitude to Foreign Religions', trans. A. Nevill, in T. Harrison (ed.), *Greeks and Barbarians*, Edinburgh: Edinburgh University Press, 172–85.

Saïd, S. (2002a), 'Greeks and Barbarians in Euripides' Tragedies: The End of Differences?', trans. A. Nevill, in T. Harrison (ed.), *Greeks and Barbarians*, Edinburgh: Edinburgh University Press, 62–100.

Saïd, S. (2002b), 'Exotic Space in *Iphigeneia in Tauris*', *Dioniso* 1: 48–61.

Sansone, D. (1975), 'The Sacrifice-Motif in Euripides' *IT*', *Transactions of the American Philological Association*, 105: 283–95.

Santelia, S. (ed.) (1991), *Charition Liberata (P. Oxy. 413)*, Bari: Levante Editori.

Schwinge, E.-R. (1968), *Die Verwending der Stichomythie in den Dramen des Euripides*, Heidelberg: Carl Winter.

Scullion, S. (2000), 'Tradition and Invention in Euripidean Aitiology', *Illinois Classical Studies* 24–25: 217–33.

Scullion, S. (2002), '"Nothing to do with Dionysos": Tragedy Misconceived as Ritual', *Classical Quarterly* 52: 102–37.

Scullion, S. (2005), 'Tragedy and Religion: The Problem of Origins', in J. Gregory (ed.), *A Companion to Greek Tragedy*, 21–37, Oxford: Blackwell Publishing.

Seaford, R. (2009), 'Aitiologies of Cult in Euripides: A Response to Scott Scullion', in J.R. Cousland and J.R. Hume (eds), *The Play of Texts and Fragments: Essays in Honour of Martin Cropp*, Leiden: Brill, 221–34.

Segal, E. (1995), '"The Comic Catastrophe": An Essay on Euripidean Comedy', in A. Griffiths (ed.), *Stage Directions: Essays in Honour of E.W. Handley*, London: Institute for Classical Studies, 46–55.

Seidensticker, B. (1971), 'Die Stichomythie', in W. Jens (ed.), *Die Bauformen der griechischen Tragödie*, Munich: Wilhelm Fink Verlag, 183–220.

Seidensticker, B. (1982), *Palintonos Harmonia: Studien zu komischen Elementen in der griechischen Tragödie*, Göttingen: Vandenhoeck & Ruprecht.

Silk, M. and J.P. Stern (1981), *Nietzsche on Tragedy*, Cambridge: Cambridge University Press.

Slater, N. (2015), 'Iphigenia Amongst the Ivies, 1915', in K. Bosher, F. Macintosh, J. McConnell and P. Rankine (eds), *The Oxford Handbook of Greek Drama in the Americas*, Oxford: Oxford University Press, 166–83.

Sommerstein, A. (1989), *Aeschylus: Eumenides*, Cambridge: Cambridge University Press.

Sommerstein, A. (2002), *Greek Drama and Dramatists*, London: Routledge.

Sourvinou-Inwood, C. (1988), *Studies in Girls' Transitions: Aspects of the Arkteia and Age Representation in Attic Iconography*, Athens: Kardamitsa.

Sourvinou-Inwood, C. (1991), *'Reading' Greek Culture: Texts and Images, Rituals and Myths*, Oxford: Oxford University Press.

Sourvinou-Inwood, C. (2003), *Tragedy and Athenian Religion*, Lanham, MD: Lexington Books.

Stamatopoulou, Z. (2012), 'Weaving Titans for Athena: Euripides and the Panathenaic *Peplos* (*Hec.* 466–74 and *IT* 218–24)', *Classical Quarterly* 62: 72–80.

Steiner, D. (2001), *Images in Mind: Statues in Archaic and Classical Greek Literature and Thought*, Princeton, NJ: Princeton University Press.

Stinton, T.W. (1976), 'Si Credere Dignum Est': Some Expressions of Disbelief in Euripides and Others', *Proceedings of the Cambridge Philological Society* 22: 60–89.

Sutton, D.F. (1980), *The Greek Satyr Play*, Meisenheim am Glan: Anton Hain.

Swift, L. (2010), *The Hidden Chorus: Echoes of Genre in Tragic Lyric*, Oxford: Oxford University Press.

Taplin, O. (1977), *The Stagecraft of Aeschylus*, Oxford: Oxford University Press.

Taplin, O. (1978), *Greek Tragedy in Action*, London: Routledge.
Thomas, R. (2000), *Herodotus in Context: Ethnography, Science and the Art of Persuasion*, Cambridge: Cambridge University Press.
Torrance, I. (2007), 'Religion and Gender in Goethe's *Iphigenie auf Tauris*', *Helios* 34(2): 177–206.
Torrance, I. (2009), 'Euripides' *IT* 72–5 and a *Skene* of Slaughter', *Hermes*, 137: 21–7.
Torrance, I. (2013), *Metapoetry in Euripides*, Oxford: Oxford University Press.
Trevelyan, H. (1981), *Goethe and the Greeks*, Cambridge: Cambridge University Press.
Trieschnigg, C. (2008), 'Iphigenia's Dream in Euripides' *Iphigenia Taurica*', *Classical Quarterly* 58: 461–78.
Tzanetou, A. (2000), 'Almost Dying, Dying Twice: Ritual and Audience in Euripides' *Iphigenia in Tauris*', *Illinois Classical Studies* 24–25: 257–72.
Vernant, J.-P. (1991), *Mortals and Immortals: Collected Essays*, edited by F. Zeitlin, Princeton, NJ: Princeton University Press.
Vernant, J.-P. (1998), *La Mort Dans Les Yeux: Figures de l'Autre en Grèce Ancienne*, Paris: Hachette Littératures.
West, M. (1992), *Ancient Greek Music*, Oxford: Oxford University Press.
West, S. (2003), '"The Most Marvellous of All Seas": The Greek Encounter with the Euxine', *Greece & Rome* 50: 151–67.
Wildberg, C. (2000), 'Piety as Service, Epiphany as Reciprocity: Two Observations on the Religious Meaning of the Gods in Euripides', *Illinois Classical Studies* 24–25: 235–56.
Wildberg, C. (2002), *Hyperesie und Epiphanie: Zur Bedeutung und Funktion der Götter in den Dramen des Euripides*, Munich: Beck.
Wilkins, J. (1990), 'The State and the Individual: Euripides' Plays of Voluntary Self-Sacrifice', in A. Powell (ed.), *Euripides, Women, and Sexuality*, London: Routledge, 177–94.
Wolff, C. (1992), 'Euripides' *Iphigenia among the Taurians*: Aetiology, Ritual, Myth', *Classical Antiquity* 11: 308–34.
Wright, M. (2005), *Euripides' Escape-Tragedies: A Study of Helen, Andromeda, and Iphigenia among the Taurians*, Oxford: Oxford University Press.

Wright, M. (2006), '*Cyclops* and the Euripidean Tetralogy', *Proceedings of the Cambridge Philological Society* 52: 23–48.

Yunis, H. (1988), *A New Creed: Fundamental Religious Beliefs in the Athenian Polis and Euripidean Drama*, Göttingen: Vandenhoeck & Ruprecht.

Zanobi, Alessandra (2010), 'From Duncan to Bausch with Iphigenia', in Fiona Macintosh (ed.), *The Ancient Dancer in the Modern World*, Oxford: Oxford University Press, 236–54.

Zeitlin, F. (2005), 'Redeeming Matricide? Euripides Rereads the *Oresteia*', in V. Pedrick and S. Oberhelman (eds), *The Soul of Tragedy: Essays on Athenian Drama*, Chicago, IL: Chicago University Press, 199–225.

Zeitlin, F. (2011), 'Sacrifices Holy and Unholy in Euripides' *Iphigenia among the Taurians*', in F. Prescendi and Y. Volokhine (eds), *Dans le Laboratoire de l'Historien des Religions: Mélanges Offerts à Philippe Borgeaud*, Geneva: Labor et Fides, 449–66.

Index

abductions and rapes 34, 87
Achilles, Thoas compared to 43–4
action 8–26
    arrival of Orestes and Pylades 9
    build-up to recognition 11–16
    Chorus lament for lost homeland 18
    Chorus sing about the arrival of the Greeks 11
    concluding scenes 24–6
    conspiracy scene 17–18
    deception scene 19–23, 63
    Iphigenia's prologue speech 8–9
    opening song 10
    reunion duet 16
    Taurian Herdsman reports capture of Greeks 10–11
    third *stasimon* – hymn in praise of Apollo 23–4
adaptations *see* reception history
aeolo-choriambic metre 11, 18, 23
Aeschylus 29
    Agamemnon 1, 16, 33, 40, 66, 71–2, 84, 115
    Eumenides 22, 36, 37, 58, 71, 96
    Libation Bearers 14–15, 17, 37, 40, 58, 74
    Oresteia trilogy 1, 17, 58, 69, 73, 75, 76, 91, 95
    Persians 57, 61
aetiologies (mythological explanations) 25–6, 80–1, 85–6, 88, 90, 91
Airs, Waters, Places (Hippocratic treatise) 67
Akalaitis, JoAnne, *The Iphigenia Cycle* 116
anagnōrisis (recognition) 26
anapaests (chanted metrical units) 11

animal sacrifices 33, 82–3
Anthesteria festival 90, *see also Choes*
antilabai (half line exchanges) 20–2
Apollo 23–4, 25, 34, 36, 51–2, 73, 74, 95–7
Archelaus 64–5
archers 60–1
Aristophanes
    Acharnians 92
    Women at the Thesmophoria 13
    Women of Lemnos 43
Aristotle 2, 4, 27, 41
    Poetics 4, 12, 26, 47
    Rhetoric 4, 41
arkteia 'festival of the bears,' 88
Artemis 74, 75, 82–4, 85–90, 93–5, 117–18
    statues 80, 84–5, 121
Athena, character 30, 46–7
    concluding epiphany 25–6, 30–1, 95–6
Athens 4–6, 47
Augustine, *Confessions* 111
axenos (inhospitable) 6–7, 67, 100

Bacon, Helen 67
Barall, Michi, *Rescue Me (A Postmodern Classic with Snacks)* 116–17
'barbarians' (*barbaroi*) 57–8, 59, 60, 62–8, 77, *see also* ethnicity; 'foreigners'; inter-ethnic relations
Bausch, Pina, *Iphigenie auf Tauris* (dance opera) 107, 115
Belfiore, Elizabeth 28
Black Sea 4–8, 86, 100
Boyle, Nicholas 114
Brauron 31, 34, 75, 80, 85–6, 88–90
Bremmer, Jan 83

captives 50, 51, 55
Carli, Gian Rinaldo, *Ifigenia in Tauri* 102
childbearing and motherhood 73–5, 89, 93
Choes ('Beakers') festival 80, 90–2
choral songs 11, 23, 29, 48–9, 50, 53, 74, 79, 96
Chorus 29, 30–1, 47–55
Cicero, *On Friendship* 109, 111
City Dionysia festival 79–80
comedy 27, 43, 87, 92
Cropp, Martin 87
customs (*nomoi*) 4, 60, 64–8, 78

dance 11, 23, 29, 79, 88, 107, 114–15, 119
date, of play 2–4
deictic pronouns 17
Delphic oracle, Apollo's takeover 51–2
Dennis, John, *Iphigenia* 105, 111, 112, 119
Diana of the Wood 66
Dionysus 72, 97, *see also Choes* festival; City Dionysia festival
dithyrambic choral songs 23
divine design and rational intellect 39, 52, 53, 92–7
dochmiac metre 16
dream, Iphigenia's 9, 11, 35, 52–3, 73, 95
Duncan, Isadora 114–15

Ekroth, Gunnel 88–9
entrapment 34–5, 55
Erotes, attributed to Lucian 111
ethnicity 57–8, 59–68
 ethnic stereotypes 30, 60–1, 76
 inter-ethnic relations in adaptations 99–109
Euripides
 Aeolus (lost tragedy) 64
 Alcestis 27, 33
 Andromache 27, 65, 96, 97

Andromeda (lost tragedy) 3
Bacchae 47, 64, 72, 97
Children of Heracles 8, 33
Cyclops 3, 22
Daughters of Pelias (lost tragedy) 3
Electra 14, 15, 22, 37, 41, 96
Hecuba 33, 69
Helen 3, 5–6 14, 23, 27, 49, 54, 102
Heracles 61, 77, 94–5
Hippolytus 13, 19, 25, 58, 69, 81, 95
Ion 8, 25, 27, 34, 47, 71, 96
Iphigenia at Aulis 1, 13, 31, 33, 34, 93
Medea 45, 53, 77
Orestes 25, 27, 37, 40, 60, 62
Suppliant Women 7–8, 33, 47, 64
Trojan Women 5, 23, 45, 51, 55, 117

female and male roles 16, 29–30, 58–9, 68–77, 117
female priesthoods 8, 12, 14, 30, 58, 62, 70–1, 138n.38
feminist responses, to the play 114–16
festivals 22, 32, 79–80, 85, 87–8, 90–2
Foley, Helene 24, 115–16
'foreigners' 57–8, 59–68, 76–8, *see also* inter-ethnic relations
friendship, male 41, 109–111, 118–19
Furies 6, 8, 36, 37–8, 39, 52, 74, 86, 90, 91, 119
Furley, William 53

Gamel, Mary-Kay, *Effie and the Barbarians* 116
gender dynamics *see also* female and male roles
 in adaptations 109–17
 in Euripides 58–9
Gluck, Christoph Willibald, *Iphigénie en Tauride* (opera) 106–7, 119

Index

gods 79–98
  Choes festival 90–2
  conflation between Iphigenia and Artemis 84–5
  divine design and rational intellect 39, 52, 53, 92–7
  Euripides' representation of 81–2
  Halai and Brauron 85–90
  human sacrifices 65, 68, 82–5, 117–18
  religious rituals 79–81
Goethe, Johann Wolfgang von, *Iphigenie auf Tauris* 102–6, 110, 112–13, 114, 115, 116, 120, 121
Goff, Barbara 6, 75, 80, 85
golden lamb 50–1
Granville-Barker, Harley, *Iphigenia in Tauris* production 107, 114
greed 50–1
Greeks 4, 57–8
  and Taurians 59–68, 76–8
Gregory, Justina 28
Guimond de la Touche, Claude, *Iphigénie en Tauride* 106, 112

Halai (Halai Araphenides) 85–8, 89–90
Hall, Edith 27, 74, 76, 99, 103–5, 107, 109–10, 116, 118–19, 121
Harrison, Tony, *Iphigenia in Crimea* (verse drama) 117
Hartigan, Karelisa 36–7
Herodotus 4, 6, 7, 34, 57, 59, 62, 65, 67, 84
  on Persians 63, 64
heroic characteristics 39–40, 42, 43, 44
heroic quests 36–7
Homer, *Iliad* 18
  Odyssey 36, 42
Homeric Hymn to Demeter 34
human sacrifices 7, 8–9, 50, 55, 59, 63–5, 68, 93–4

Artemis and Iphigenia 82–5
  in reception history 103, 108, 117–18

iambic trimetres 3–4, 16
Ifigenia w Taurydzie, Centre for Theatre Practices 'Gardzienice,' production 120–1
Ingleheart, Jennifer 100, 110
inhospitable (*axenos*) 6–7, 67, 100
inter-ethnic relations 99–109
Iphigenia, character 30, 31–6, 69–70, 71–7, 82–5, 93–4

katabasis (heroic descent to underworld) 36–7
Kertész, Imre, *The Pathseeker* 105
korai statues 114
kyrios ('validator'/male guardian) 68, 70

La Grange-Chancel, François Joseph de, *Oreste et Pylade* 102, 111, 119
letters 85, 100
  Iphigenia's 12–14, 76, 130n.24
line-by-line exchange (*stichomythia*) 10, 19
Lloyd-Jones, Hugh 89
Lucian, *Toxaris* 110, *see also Erotes*

madness 37–40, 41, 60, 86
male and female roles 16, 29–30, 68–77, 117
male friendship 41, 109–111, 118–19
Mastronarde, Donald 28, 53
McClure, Laura 72, 84
McInerney, Jeremy 87
McLaughlin, Ellen, *Iphigenia and Other Daughters* 115–16
mēchanē (stage crane) 25
Menander, *The Litigants* 87
messenger speeches 24
metabolas (extreme reversals) 26–7

metrical structure 3–4, 10, 11, 16, 18, 23
Mirto, Maria 89
motherhood and childbearing 73–5, 89, 93
mythological explanations (aetiologies) 25–6, 80–1, 85–6, 88, 90, 91

nature (*physis*) vs nurture (*nomos*) 64
noble characteristics 38, 39, 40–2, 44, 103
nomoi (customs/laws) 4, 60, 64–8, 78
Nowra, Louis, *The Golden Age* 108

opera 102, 106–7, 111, 114, 119
Orestes, character 30, 36–43
Ovid, *Letters from the Black Sea* 100–1
 Tristia 100–1, 117–18

Panathenaea festival 22, 32, 80
Papadopoulou, Thalia 95
Parker, Laetitia 11, 45
parodos (opening song) 10, 15
Pausanias 87
peripeteia (reversal of fortune) 26
Persians 57, 62, 63, 64, 76
piety 30, 45, 46, 55, 63, 119
Pindar, *Olympian* 1, 94
Plautus, *The Captives* 27
plot 1–2, 3, 95
 tragic plot 26–8
Plutarch, *Life of Pericles* 4
 Life of Themistocles 83
Plynteria ('Washing') festival, 22, 85
pollution 21–2, 23, 36, 45, 55–6, 89, 91–2, 93, *see also* purification rituals
Post, Levi 107
'pre-romance' play 27
props 1, 13–15, 19, 22–3

purification rituals 17, 19, 21–2, 36, 45, 46, 53, 62, 74, 85
 City Dionysia festival 79, 80
Pylades, character 30, 36–43
Pythia 70–1

Racine, Jean 102, 103
rapes and abductions 34, 87
rational intellect and divine design 39, 52, 53, 92–7
reception history 99–121
 gender dynamics 109–117
 inter-ethnic relations 99–109
 religion 117–21
recognition tokens 14–16
religion 79–98, *see also* animal sacrifices; customs; human sacrifices
 festivals 22, 79–80, 87–8, 90–2
 Halai and Brauron 75, 80, 85–90
 in reception history 117–21
religious piety 30, 45, 46, 55, 63, 119
reversal of fortune (*peripeteia*) 26–7
Reyes, Alfonso, *Ifigenia Cruel* 108
Ritsos, Yannis, 'The Return of Iphigenia,' 120
rituals 79–98, *see also* animal sacrifices; customs; human sacrifices
 festivals 22, 79–80, 87–8, 90–2
 Halai and Brauron 75, 80, 85–90
Rucellai, Giovanni, *Oreste* 102, 111, 119

Saïd, Suzanne 57
Sansone, David 28
scenes *see* action
Schlegel, Johann Elias, *Orest und Pylades* 111
sculptures 84–5, 114, *see also* statues
setting, of play 4–8
sexual content, lack of 55
slavery 50, 51, 55
song *see* choral songs

sophists 57–8
Sophocles 29
   Ajax 40, 86, 117
   Electra 15, 37, 115
   Oedipus the King 26
   Philoctetes 68
Sourvinou-Inwood, Christiane, 74–5
Spinoza, Baruch 114
stage crane (*mēchanē*) 25
stasimon (choral song) 11
statues 8, 19, 22, 79, 84–5, 87, 114, 120–1
stichomythia (line-by-line exchange) 10, 19
Strabo 6
strophic pairs 11, 23, 50, 51
supplication 17–18, 131n32
Swift, Laura 49

Tantalus myth 66, 93, 94
Taurian Herdsman, character 30, 45–6
Taurian Messenger, character 30, 45–6
Taurians 4, 7, 46, 86–7, 99–101
   and Greeks 59–68, 76–8
Tauropolia festival 87–8

Thoas, character 30, 43–5, 59, 60, 61, 63–4
tokens, recognition 14–15
Trader Horn (book and film) 107
tragicomedy 27
tragic plots 26–8
tribes 62, 65, *see also* Taurians
Trieschnigg, Caroline 52–3, 95
Tyche play (based on luck) 27
Tzanetou, Angeliki 88

Vaubertrand, Jean-Baptiste-Claude 102

wealth acquisition 50–1
Winckelmann, Johann Joachim 113–14
women 68–73, 74–7, 89, 112–14, 115, *see also* female and male roles; female priesthoods
Wright, Matthew 3, 28, 55

Xenophon, *Spartan Constitution* 87
xenos (reciprocal guest-friendship) 65–7, 103

Zanobi, Alessandra 115
Zeitlin, Froma 89, 95, 136n.19

www.ingramcontent.com/pod-product-compliance
Lightning Source LLC
Chambersburg PA
CBHW051646230426
43669CB00013B/2464